SUNDERLAND F.C. 1951 -

from the archives o

GW00836295

11/2+
£1·00

Charles Buchan's
FOOTBALL MONTHLY

Edited and written by: Andrew S. Dolloway

MMP

Copyright 2021 Max Media Publishing Ltd
First published in Great Britain by: Max Media Publishing Ltd 2021

ISBN 978-1-9169011-6-2

www.maxmediapublishing.com

Max Media Publishing Limited
49-51 Bancroft Lane, Mansfield, Notts. NG18 5LG

Edited and written by **Andrew Dolloway**

Charles Buchan's Football Monthly content reproduced with permission from
Max Media Publishing

Associate Design by **Simon Meakin at In House Design**, Mansfield, Notts.
Printed by Max Media Publishing, United Kingdom.

Every effort has been made to fulfil requirements with regard to reproducing copyright material.
The publishers will be glad to rectify any omissions at the earliest opportunity.

All rights reserved.

No part of this publication may be reproduced, stored in a retrieval system, or transmitted, in any form or by any means
without the prior written consent of the publisher, nor be otherwise circulated in any form of binding or cover other than
that in which it is published and without a similar condition being imposed on the subsequent purchaser.

STOKOES
STARS

WEMBLEY
73

WELL DONE SUNDERLAND

DAIMLER

NCN 77L

Con

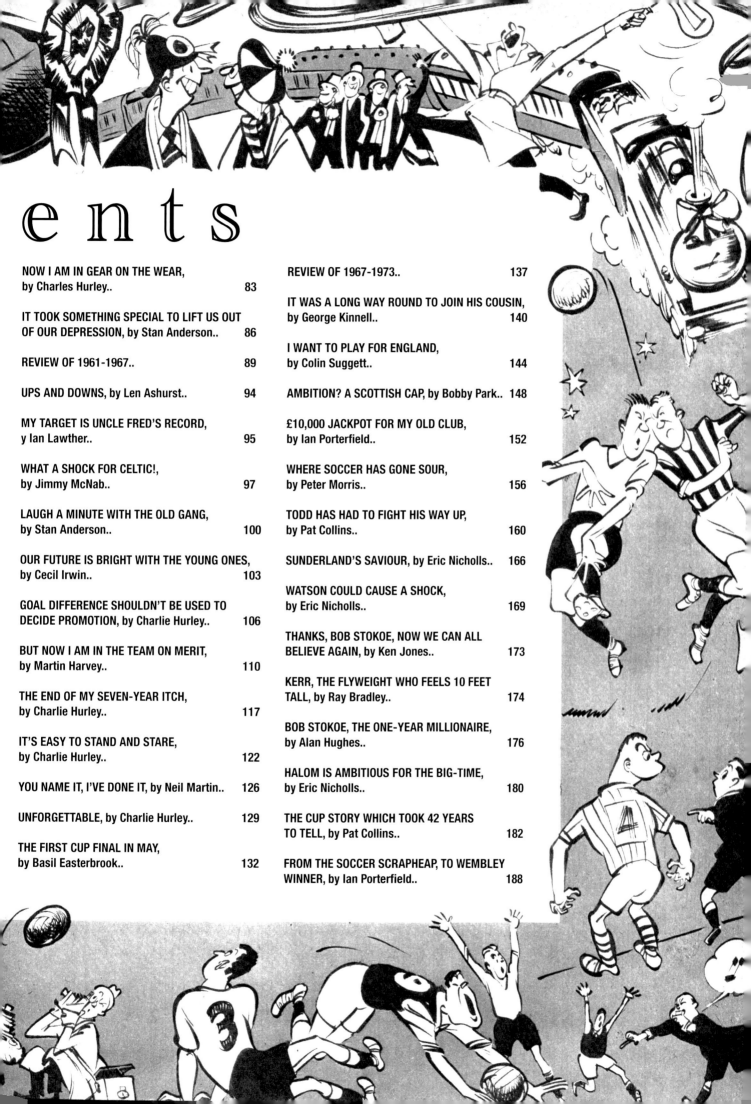

ents

CHARLES BUCHAN'S
FOOTBALL
SUNDERLAND
1951-1973

PETER COLLINS

PETER MORRIS

JOHN THOMPSON

BBC

ROLAND ALLEN

CHARLES BUCHAN

JOHN MACADAM

NORMAN ACKLAND

Meet the Charles Buchan's Football Monthly Team

MMP

Introduction

The Charles Buchan's Football Monthly story.

The peak in football's popularity came in the late 1940's when attendances in England and Scotland reached over 47 million as a war weary population flocked to soccer as an escape from rationing and the greyness of everyday life.

The standard of the game might not have been high, some players were exhausted after serving their country in far flung parts of the world, others were youngsters with little experience, whilst some never returned to the game at all. Grounds weren't fit for purpose and many teams had to beg for clothing vouchers to even kit the team out.

It was into this background that Charles Buchan's Football Monthly was launched. As paper shortages eased and industry returned to normal, the time was right for the national game to get the periodical it deserved.

The first issue hit the newsstands in September 1951 and featured the legendary Stanley Matthews in colour on the front cover.

The magazine was the brainchild of Charles Buchan, John Thompson and Joe Sarl and was aimed at the growing number of football fans who were disenchanted with the quality and variety of football writing available at that time. Of course every town had its 'Pink Un' or 'Green Un' reporting on the local scene but football fans were crying out for, not only their own magazine, but also some colour after the drab war years. There were of course a variety of Sports Magazines that did feature football but also cricket and boxing, plus there would be a lot of space put aside for systems on how to win the 'Football Pools', a post war Phenomenon, followed by many

with no interest in the game itself, but there was nothing dedicated to football alone.

Charles Buchan was no mere figurehead, an esteemed and highly respected player with Sunderland and Arsenal until he retired in the mid 1920's, he then moved effortlessly into journalism for the News Chronicle, before also becoming a national figure on the BBC Light Service, commenting on football matters.

Charles Buchan was also widely travelled, having not only served with distinction in the First World War, but also having been on numerous overseas tours as a reporter. Although not a controversial figure, he held strong views on football and he particularly wanted to increase the status of the players themselves, many who were still treated as serfs by their clubs. Charlie as he was affectionately known, hated discrimination wherever he encountered it and the magazine often sponsored under privileged youngsters from around the world. Charlie's watchword was 'grand', games were 'grand', players were 'grand' and the game would always be Soccer with a capital S in Football Monthly.

His partners in the venture were John Thompson and Joe Sarl. John who was the 'de facto' editor of the magazine, also worked for the Daily Mirror and Joe, although not a big football fan was considered the business brains behind the magazine.

The first offices were a couple of pokey rooms on the Strand in London and as John Thompson recalled many years later, 'Money was tight, we were hard up for furniture, in fact to begin with we only had one proper chair

and that was usually reserved for guests. There was a crack in the window and the sound of buses trundling up and down the road outside added to the soundtrack. In winter, that office was freezing, it was a usual sight to see us all working in our hats and scarves whilst Charlie always had a pipe on the go'.

The first issue was priced at 1/6d, expensive for the time, so it was not aimed at the lower end of the market. (This price also ensured that readers cherished the magazine and it instantly became very collectable).

In order that the magazine had good content for its first issue, many favours were pulled in from friends. Raich Carter discussed his new role as player manager and there was even an article by the Marquess of Londonderry on his recent conversion to football. (It was after finding himself sitting next to the Arsenal chairman at a dinner he attended at Buckingham Palace.) The highbrow tone continued with a short story from J.B. Priestley, this was clearly going to be no ordinary football magazine.

After a tentative beginning, Football Monthly quickly found its own voice. There were always lots of interesting stories and photographs about clubs and players, not always the expected stars, as many of the lesser lights were also featured. These stories were often flavoured with war anecdotes or 'rags to riches' tales along the lines of 'pithead to football hero' and from the beginning Scottish football was well covered, although it always made an extra effort if there was a Rangers' picture, you could always be sure there would be

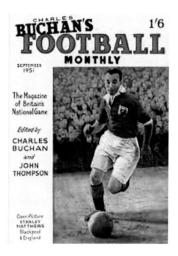

a Celtic one to even it up. The writing and design always aspired to quality and innovation. This was reflected in the use of colour images from the start, although these often had a surreal quality about them as the colour was painstakingly added by an artist to a black and white image to create the desired effect.

From the very early days the contributors to Football Monthly could be considered a 'motley crew', coming from a hugely varied background.

Lesley Yates who was to be the longest serving contributor to the magazine, primarily supplied fillers, that is small articles to fill spaces that eventually became the 'soccer sideshow' feature, these quirky stories often re-edited and used again if time was pressing.

Peter Morris was the feature writer and sub editor who came to the fore in the 1960's. Brian Glanville who at the age of only twenty, produced a mammoth work that contained the details of over 1,300 players, that was serialized over six months and he later contributed many articles about the foreign game.

The magazine tried to introduce its readers to the wider game, this was not an easy job as foreigners were often viewed with suspicion for their funny customs and names. No Stans, Bills or Harrys amongst them and whilst Britain might not always beat them at football, at least we could be assured that we would never sink so low as having our supporters caged in, or police resorting to baton charges and tear gas. There was a great picture of John Thompson in South America with his typewriter on his lap next to a moat and a wire fence.

Other contributors included Clifford Webb, also editor of the Sporting Record and jolly fine company at the bar. Norman Ackland who covered the amateur scene (this at a time when the Amateur Cup Final drew 100,000 spectators to Wembley), came across as 'old school' in his striped blazer but in reality he had a checkered past. He once worked as a bookies runner in Dublin, then survived Dunkirk, before taking up journalism. He was also renowned for his way with the ladies and one of his sons was Joss Ackland, who went on to have a fine career in TV and film.

Then there was Pat Collins who joined the staff in 1960 and later took over as editor from John Thompson, overseeing the magazine's growth in the years up to the 1966 World Cup Final and finally John Macadam with his distinctive handlebar moustache. As with many journalists of that time he was a confirmed batchelor, preferring to spend his time swapping anecdotes in the pub. He also saw action as an RAF pilot during the war on D Day. He loved his football but he was never happier than when he was in the company of prizefighters in Chicago and New York.

These were the characters who gave this magazine its distinctive flavour, an eclectic bunch of rounded men who knew football was important but not at the expense of everything else and when the magazine had to deal with tragedy such as the Munich air crash or the Ibrox tragedy it was handled with style.

By 1958 the magazine's circulation had risen to 107,000 and the partners felt confident enough to move into new premises on Fleet Street, ironically on the same site where the Football League had been formed in the old Andertons Hotel. Charles Buchan's Publications also now decided to expand its interests. Since 1953 they had published a Christmas annual, a huge success and now branched out into a variety of specialist titles covering cycling, gardening and cine cameras amongst others.

In one year alone after moving, circulation increased by another 20,000. Everything seemed to be progressing nicely until news came that Charles Buchan had collapsed and died whilst on vacation in the South of France. He was 68. A memorial service was held at the journalists church of St Brides, Fleet Street and was attended by hundreds of Charlie's friends including stars from football and journalism.

Even after the death of its founder, the magazine went from strength to strength, peaking at 200.000 sales in the year England won the World Cup. The Boys Club membership reached over 100,000 and popular features such as programme swap and request a pen pal were regular features for years and attracted young boys who would one day go on to make their own names. Barry Fry collected and exchanged autographs even after he joined Manchester United, in 1959 a thirteen year old John Motson had a letter published, whilst author Sebastian Faulks was the writer of the Star Letter in September 1967, earning him a three guinea postal order. The readership was as varied as the writers.

Although the articles were great, so were the pictures. Many older players still remember the hordes of kids with multiple copies of the magazine demanding their signature. By now each issue had up to eight colour pages and often a double page team spread, plus lots of great black and white action shots.

After the highs came the lows, changing fashions may explain the eventual demise of the magazine as the editors seemed loathe to alter a winning formula, but by the end of the 1960's the format seemed tired and dated. The magazine was not helped by the decision of the new publishers, Longacre Press to publish a sister magazine, the weekly Goal, basically a weekly version that promised a whole new fresh approach and even had Goal 'dolly birds'. To the younger readers this approach worked and as sales of Football Monthly fell, so did editorial values and there were more and more filler articles and adverts.

There were several attempts by the publishers to re-energise the magazine, including dropping the name Charles Buchan from the title in 1971, after all who was he to the younger generation? Worse still there was another rival on the scene in the form of 'Shoot', a magazine that was the equivalent of ITV's Magpie compared to the BBC's Blue Peter.

Football Monthly staggered on even being printed for twelve months in smaller digest form until it was finally halted in 1974, a victim of changing times, but for twenty years it lead the way in football coverage and held a special place in the hearts of soccer followers everywhere.

Even now, forty years on from the magazine's demise, no-one with a love of the game can fail to be charmed whenever they see a copy of Charles Buchan's Football Monthly.

In this book we have tried to capture the spirit and ethos of that timeless magical publication. I hope we have succeeded.

Charles Buchan's 1951-56 SUNDERLAND

Bill Murray

As football resumed after the war, every club was to encounter obstacles along the way, but for Sunderland, many of theirs were to be self inflicted, and would turn out to have huge ramifications for the club for the following 30 years.

As manager Bill Murray considered his options in 1946, he was lucky on one hand that no players had died in combat, many of them seeing the war out in 'protected' industries such as the coal mines, but the players he was left with, were either ageing, or affected by their war-time experiences, meaning realistically they had to be replaced by local talent, or with locally born players who had drifted away but could be encouraged to return.

There was also the Raich Carter conundrum. A supremely talented footballer, Raich wanted a long term contract that would give him security, and also reflect his service to the club. The Board refused, and so he was allowed to leave, joining Derby County, in the area where his wife had gone to see out the war. The fee, a paltry £6,000.

The player ostensibly signed to replace his star quality, albeit several years later, was Len Shackleton, an outspoken mercurial talent. He made his debut away at Derby in February 1948, with Raich Carter in the opposition ranks. Sunderland keeper Johnny Mapson was reported as saying: 'Don't worry about their number 8, let him shoot.' The result Derby 5 Sunderland 1, and four goals for Carter!

The signing of Len Shackleton for £20,000 from Newcastle can be seen as the starting point for the period when Sunderland became known as the 'Bank of England team'. Vast amounts of money, especially

for a provincial club, would be spent on transfer fees, and more importantly on signing on payments and wages, despite there being strict Football Association rules governing this.

Huge crowds had filled the coffers, meaning that the club had plenty of cash available to splash out, and after a flirtation with relegation in 1948, it was deemed essential that better players were brought in to avoid that catastrophe. But it was really the following season, after the club went out of the F.A. Cup to non-league Yeovil Town, that the Directors, after an intense meeting, began a spending spree never seen before in British Football.

In came Ivor Broadis from Carlisle United, considered to be one of the biggest talents in the game, followed quickly by Tommy Wright from Partick Thistle. At first it worked, huge crowds continued to flock to Roker Park, and the team surged to the top of the League, eventually only losing out on the title by one point. Three successive defeats in April proved to be their undoing.

The directors and Bill Murray, were convinced that the strategy would work, so

they carried on. Under a new chairman, E.W. (Ted) Ditchburn, a local furniture manufacturer, money was to be no obstacle to returning the Wearsiders to the pinnacle of English football.

In came centre-forward Trevor Ford from Aston Villa for a club record £30,000, and he immediately won fans over with three goals on his home debut, but the suspicions of the authorities were raised when the player wrote in a newspaper article that he had chosen Sunderland because: 'Of their offer of a house, and a job outside football.' The F.A. decided that the player had asked for more than the £10 signing on fee that he was entitled to, and fined him £100, the figure he had been paid by the newspaper for his story.

Ford's time at Sunderland was not a glorious one, Len Shackleton sarcastically remarked that the F.A. fine was his highlight, but that was unfair because the player had contributed 70 goals in his 117 League and Cup games, plus the club recouped £29,500 when they sold him to Aston Villa

But the fact was, in the four seasons that the player spent at Roker Park, they finished, 12th, 12th, 9th and 18th. But surely this underachievement reflected as badly on all the players?

The big money signings just kept on coming. Billy Bingham for £9,000 from Glentoran in 1951, another £20,000 to Third Lanark for George Aitken.

Money was also spent off the pitch. Floodlights were installed in the winter of 1952, and this allowed the occasional friendly against Continental opposition.

The team made a wonderful start to the 1952-53 season, leading the table on January 3rd after beating Arsenal, but

Action from the F.A. Cup semi-final against Manchester City

after Trevor Ford broke his leg, they went 12 games without a win, dropping like a stone to ninth place, where they eventually finished.

Once more the cheque book came out, and the club spent an unprecedented £62,000 in twelve days on three players. First Scottish international keeper Jimmy Cowan joined for £8,000, then Arsenal were persuaded to release Ray Daniel for £27,000, before finally a further £26,000 was spent on the England left-winger Billy Elliott. For this period, these were stupendous sums of money.

Even then the club weren't finished. December saw Cardiff's Ken Chisholm join for £15,000, followed a month later by Ted Purdon from Birmingham City for another £15,000, signed to replace the departed Trevor Ford.

When you include a couple of other lesser signings, the club had spent in total, £110,000 on new players, and that was just on the transfer fees. Yet even with this array of talent, they were knocked out of the Cup 2-0 at home by Doncaster Rovers, and finished the season only five places off the bottom of the League. What went wrong? Many thought that so many big name signings had ruined team spirit. Perhaps they were playing as individuals

rather than for the team, though some fans were even prepared to accept a lack of success, because of the glamour and entertainment attached to the club.

Trevor Ford

What of the players signed, how had they shaped up individually? The worst signing undoubtedly was keeper Cowan, who after shipping lots of goals, was hurriedly sent back to Third Lanark. Ray Daniel had a torrid first season, the caustic wit of Shackleton again caught it: 'Remember that bad spell you had Ray? The one from September to April.'

Season 1954-55 was the closest they got to achieving their ambition of winning the title, and could in fact have been a 'double'

winning year. The defence had tightened up, but then inexplicably the forward line stopped scoring. The redoubtable Billy Elliott, the most expensive player in the forward line, unbelievable failed to score a single goal in the whole season!

They went top after Christmas, and were always in contention, but a lack of goals was to cost them dearly both in the League, and the F.A. Cup, where they went out at the semi-final stage, 1-0 to Manchester City, thereby robbing the public of a Tyneside-Wearside final. They eventually finished fourth, but only four points behind Chelsea, who won the title with the lowest number of points for years.

Hopes were high the following season once more, and supporters were encouraged by the start that Sunderland made, going top, after winning at Tottenham in late October. But the good form disappeared. An unbelievable 8-2 defeat at Luton Town, precipitating a slide down the table.

As usual, the only answer always seemed to be, 'buy another player'. This was panicked, ill-thought out and directionless.

Worse still, the chickens were about to come home to roost, as the club's flagrant disregard of the game's financial rules, was about to be exposed

MANCHESTER CITY

He might not be everyone's cup of tea, but
Len Shackleton, the **Sunderland schemer**,
certainly knows where the back of the net is.

BOLTON WANDERERS

Foundation stones

by WILLIE

It is said that the late Herbert Chapman, still referred to by people older than I am as about the best of the managers of recent times, built up Huddersfield Town and then Arsenal in that way.

He decided for instance, that his Arsenal team would play the third full-back game, so he got a six foot fellow to do the stopping act, and followed him with another big strong stopper in our friend Bernard Joy. He got Alex James, a very clever forward, not to score goals, but to make goals for the other forwards. Men to play to a pattern, that's one way.

The other way, which may be equally effective, again I wouldn't know, is to find a sufficiency of really good players and to weld them into a team. It may well be, and this seems to be the impression held by old-timers still connected with Sunderland, that this was the way 'the team of all talents' was built up. Let us, however, leave these, and possibly other methods of team-building get down to the demands of current play. Of course we want a team with a talented player in each position on the field.

The first real move in the erection of a stable structure is the foundation. So we come to the foundation ston3es of a good team and if in this connection I talk mainly about top class clubs and top class players, don't forget that the principle applies to your village team as well as to the First Division champions or cup winners.

I have no doubts in my own mind as to the players who can most properly be referred to

moved, two or three players should be dropped and so on.

Just recently the managerial chair of a First Division club was left vacant. The variety of people who thought that they were shaped just right to fit into that important managerial chair amazed me. 'Cooks son, duke's son, son of a belted earl,' that is the quotation which best fit's the all-round nature of the applicants. Some of them had no more real acquaintance with a football than that of throwing it back to the field when it was kicked to their place on the terrace. But they knew all right; they imagined it was oh so easy. Silly of course, but true nevertheless.

Where is the scratch mark for this business of starting to build up a good football team? Quite frankly, I don't know the answer to that one, and maybe different answers would be given by even the most successful team managers. It strikes me that there are two main starting places. The builder might have a mental picture of the sort of football he expected the team which he was beginning to build to play.

Ever so many people are fully confident that they are quite capable of building a good football team. They think they even know better how to do that, even than folk who make a speciality of the job. This or that side loses a few matches; it has a bad time. The letters flow in, not by ones or twos, but by scores, from supporters of the side telling the manager just what he should do, or what he has done which is all wrong This or that player should be

of the best teams
WATSON
Sunderland and England half-back

as the foundation stones of any good team, as the game is played today. First come the wing half-backs. It is there, first and foremost, that good teams are made. An old saying used to run something like this: 'Show me your half-back line and I will tell you what sort of team you have.' That old tag might be revised, to fit in with modern methods, on this line, 'Let me see your wing half-backs, etc.'

The wing half-backs are not picked out by me as the foundation stones because I have played quite a lot at wing half, although I have no objection to any footballer, no matter where he plays, believing that his is the most important position on the field. It's a thought which leads to the top.

Consider what the wing halves must do, or what they should be capable of doing. They must of course, have the skill, the determination, the will to get the ball from the other fellows and to stop them from carrying out their schemes. Even if they are beaten they must get back in another effort to secure that ball. Having got the ball, the success or failure, of the team depends to a large extent on what they do with it. Those pals in front need the ball, the man in the best position to receive it and to report progress must be served with it.

Wing half-backs we call them. Do you remember the story of the fellow who went to his first match asking his friends: "How long has a chap to play half-back before he becomes a full-back?" The real answer is that at times the wing half-back is a full-back, and that he could also be given another name which would fit, a half-forward. He is also that.

It is surely not without significance that the captains of last season's Cup Final teams, Joe Harvey and Harry Johnson, were wing half-backs and while we are about it, the fact may be added that the Cup winners of each of the two previous seasons, Arsenal and Wolves, were also captained by a wing half, Joe Mercer and Billy Wright respectively.

One has only to think of half the things Billy Wright has done for his country and for his club in the last few years to realise what that sor of foundation stone means to the whole structure. When at his best, I should say that Billy Wright plays the ball about twice, in any ordinary match, to every once by any of his team-mates. Now back, now up, always there; ever in the game, no matter where it is being played.

For two or three seasons back, Tottenham Hotspur have been a great team. They have good players in each position on the field; the First Division championship can't be won by a side carrying passengers. But surely the main props of the building have been wing half-backs Billy Nicholson and Ronnie Burgess. They are the sort of players who make good forwards better and who make the job of the full-backs

Tommy Trump says:-
"A winner on all grounds"
DOUBLE ACE
The ACE of cigarettes
10 for **1/3½.**

so much easier. So one could continue the story of wing half-backs who do much to make their teams into good ones.

Already, in this team we are building, we have two main foundation stones, according to my view. After these come the inside wing forwards. These may differ in method and in the things they do, but they are of only slightly less importance than the wing half-backs. They must be workers too, non stop ninety minute players, fetching, carrying, feeding. If, in addition to all this, they can still find the energy to be up to bang one into the net from time to time, all the better. Of course it's a big order.

Did anybody ever se Wilf Mannion come off the field, no matter how cold the day, with other than a wet shirt? Billy Steel is another who can also be taken as a pattern. There is another standard by which their importance can be judged. It is the inside forwards for whom the really big prices are paid, the record transfer fees even. Jackie Sewell made a wonderful difference to Sheffield Wednesday's return in the latter part of the season. After that he gave the people of Australia a clear-cut idea of the all round part of an inside-forward. Rightly or wrongly then, I have laid the foundation stones on which to build my team. Wing half-backs, and inside-forwards. If I had in my imaginary team world-beaters in those positions, I don't think I should have to stay awake at night worrying unduly about whether the building would stand up in face of the stormiest opposition.

THE news stunned all of us! It was the greatest shock of our young lives. We felt that the world had come to an end . . .

For a week the school nearly went on strike. The masters were as much concerned about this sensational affair as we were, and they were only too eager to discuss it.

Charlie Buchan, captain of Sunderland Football Club, had been signed by the mighty Arsenal. To us he was almost a demi-god on the Soccer field.

His popularity was terrific; for in Sunderland there are only two topics to discuss—Soccer and shipbuilding.

There is, perhaps, no town in the country of its size—200,000—which is so football-mad, and at that time, in the twenties, Soccer was Charlie Buchan and Charlie Buchan was Sunderland.

Repeatedly we had seen him at Roker Park, almost carrying the team on his shoulders to victory, heading in wonderful goals from crosses by Harry Martin, and also dribbling half the length of the field . . . Wonderful solo efforts which set the crowd roaring as he finished them off with beautiful, unstumbling shots.

So that morning, when one of the masters came in and told us Charlie was leaving for ever, we felt that Sunderland was finished as a great club.

At the start of every lesson after that, the moment the master entered he would barely have written the name of the subject on the board before one of the boys would pipe up: "What do you think of the Buchan transfer, sir?"

He would immediately forget about geography, science, or whatever the subject was, and talk explosively, wrathfully, and even informatively, about the whole affair, winding up with some of his memories of Charlie's feats.

We even wanted to send a protest to the Football League, but as the masters pointed out, it would do no good at all. The transfer had taken place and that was the end of it!

So it went on for at least a week, work forgotten and only Charlie's departure being tantamount. He was probably the most popular player in the town, and there are still many of the older fans whose faces light up with pleasure at the grand, far-off days, when his name is mentioned.

There were one or two groaners, however, men who used to howl abuse at him, even when his play was sparkling.

I remember the opening game against Liverpool, one season in the '20s. Charlie got a "hat-trick" that day, but the moment he appeared on the field a red-headed chap in front of me, wearing a cloth cap and muffler, started screaming abuse at him:

"*Get off the field. You are nowt but a great big lass. Get off the field!*" And similar abusive expressions.

Charlie went on to score the "hat-trick," and one of the goals was one of the cheekiest I have ever seen.

The goalkeeper was none other than the famous Elisha Scott, of Liverpool, who played in so many internationals for Ireland. No goalkeeper of his day had such a strong pair of hands as 'Lisha.

The game had not been on long when Buchan shot. Scott held the ball, but for a fraction of a second, Charlie stood back on one foot and with the other coolly flicked the ball out of Scott's hand into the net.

It was all done in a flash and the crowd roared their heads off.

They were, of course, cheering Charlie, but the old boy beside me went on abusing him even after Charlie had scored two more fine goals, leading, if my memory serves me right, to a 3—0 victory.

Even as Charlie was leaving the field, the old boy was still abusing him.

When we were not running errands to get tanners to get into the Boys' entrance at Roker Park, to watch Charlie play, we used to run down from the school and press our noses against the windows of the sports shop in the town which Charlie kept in partnership with Amos Lowings, a Durham County cricketer.

CHARLIE WAS THEIR DARLIN'

We would wait for hours in the hope of seeing Charlie taking something out of the window.

Having seen him, we would hop off happily, always talking about what a great player he was and about his latest exploits.

The Newcastle United players used to annoy us because, perhaps out of jealousy, perhaps out of sheer rivalry, they would always point out that Charlie was a great club centre-forward, but he was a dead loss in internationals.

They said that he was far too great a genius and individualist to fit into an England side. In fact, people elsewhere in the country thought this, and the selectors did, too, because every now and then he was dropped, although I personally had never seen him play a bad game.

He was always in top form and the fact that a man is sometimes judged to be too brilliant to reap all the international honours he deserves is probably the craziest argument I have ever heard expressed in Soccer.

However, Sunderland have the habit every score of years or so of developing a genius like Charlie. There is one in the present Sunderland side—Len Shackleton.

Although I am a great admirer of him, I don't think he is quite so popular in the town as Charlie then was.

If the day comes for Shackleton to leave Sunderland, I doubt if my old school, or any other in the district, is likely to stage a "sit-down strike" . . . just because a man is being transferred.

COULD IT HAPPEN HERE?

ONE of the most unusual decisions in the annals of Soccer history was handed down by the National (U.S.A.) Indoor League, when Referee Eli Korer submitted his report after the game between the Lions and Necaxa, and reversed his decision made on the field of play.

The much-talked-about incident occurred with three minutes of play left in the Lions-Necaxa tussle with the score tied at 0—0. The Lions were awarded a free-kick for dangerous play, and Dan Stefanovich scored direct with a sizzling shot from 25 yards out. Referee Korer disallowed the goal, thinking that it was an Indirect Free-Kick. According to Indoor Rules set up especially for the tournament, all dangerous play fouls are punishable with a Direct Free-Kick.

After the game Korer admitted his mistake, and reported that the goal should have been allowed. League officials were of opinion that the Lions were therefore entitled to the goal, but that Necaxa should be given the opportunity of playing the balance of three minutes, thus giving them time to adopt tactics for a last-minute attempt to erase the one-goal deficit. The three minutes were replayed with no further scoring.

League officials wish it to be known that their action was only taken because the referee admitted his error, thereby changing the result of the game in his official report. In no circumstances would the league reverse a referee's decision on its own accord.

(*National Soccer News, Chicago*)

LEN SHACKLETON

Sunderland F.C.

CHARLES BUCHAN'S
FOOTBALL
MONTHLY

1/6

DECEMBER
1952

Inside:

MY STORY
by
JACK
CHISHOLM

CHELSEA'S
TASK
by
TED DRAKE

THEY SAY
I'M TOUGH
by
SEAN FALLON

AND SOCCER'S
MOST VIVID
PICTURES

Edited by
CHARLES BUCHAN
and
JOHN THOMPSON

TREVOR FORD
Sunderland and Wales

TREVOR FORD, THE RED DRAGON FROM PARADISE PARK

A FOOTBALL career which was to mean purgatory to many opponents began in a park named Paradise.

The nine-year-old boy would be taken there by his father. They would carry a football, a boot and a gym shoe, and in the park the boy would put the boot on his shaky left foot and the gym shoe on his trusty right foot.

To-day Trevor Ford, of Sunderland and Wales, probably the world's greatest centre-forward, realises how much he owes to those early lessons in Paradise Park, Swansea.

" My father would throw the ball at me time after time," he recalls. " The right foot was the natural and easy one for me to use, but as it hurt to kick the full-size ball with the light gym shoe, I soon got into the habit of using the better protected left foot."

It is Ford's two-footedness which adds so much to his menace. The big Welshman lets fly without pause. There is no check in his stride, however awkwardly the ball may reach him.

He knows that in other positions a one-footed player may conceal his deficiency. A centre-forward, perpetually crowded by the stopper centre-half, often with little space in which to manoeuvre, and no time to spare at all, must be equally proficient with both feet.

Ford's speed off the mark, his fearlessness and his honest vigour, his unusual mobility and powerful kicking make him an opponent who has earned respect from many rival defences.

He has to be watched carefully whether play is near him or not, for his pace and wholeheartedness enable him to take chances which would be out of the reach of lesser men.

Transferred from Swansea Town to Aston Villa for £10,000 in January, 1947, Ford had already played twice for the national team he was to represent so often.

As a Villa player he played for Wales on ten more occasions before moving to Sunderland in exchange for £29,500 in October, 1950.

He is now an established member of the Welsh attack, and contributed generously to the championship success of last season.

Acknowledged to be a skilful footballer everywhere the game is played, Ford still has his critics. His style provokes strong feeling.

I have heard him booed bitterly. But, after the game concerned I have heard no complaints from the men he has opposed on the field.

There was the occasion when Jimmy Cowan, Scotland's goalkeeper, was injured in a collision with him. Cowan later received a letter from Ford in which the Welshman apologised for unwittingly being the cause of the injury.

And Cowan's reply was typical of the manner in which men play a man's sport. He said that he realised it had been accidental, that it was all in the game.

Ford's uncompromising attitude is that the giving and taking of hard knocks are within the essential spirit of football, that without the robust shoulder-charge the game would lose much of its appeal, both to players and spectators.

Yet he recognises the necessity for abolishing the foul play which seldom brings the disapproval of the crowd because it is done slyly and with cunning.

In days in which goalkeepers are often excessively protected by referees from the hurly-burly they once experienced, Ford's treatment of them is bound to provoke controversy. But his argument is unanswerable.

" When the goalkeeper is in possession of the ball, with both feet on the ground," he says, " I am perfectly entitled to charge him, either to get the ball from him, or to bundle him and the ball over the goal-line."

Until the rules are changed—and let us

" What, carry him off and have his muddy boots all over our nice clean stretcher ! "

hope they are left alone—Ford is within his rights. That cannot be disputed.

As he has said : " Shoulder charging is an inherent feature of the game. It has been so from the start of football, and I hope it will continue while I am still actively concerned with it."

Ford's attitude might perhaps be dismissed more easily if he belonged purely to the " get stuck in " brigade. But Ford is regarded, even by his sternest critics, as a footballer of singular craftsmanship.

I have even heard it said : " I can't understand why Ford needs to be so robust when his skill would permit him to baffle opponents without using all that vigour as well."

Ford provides the answer when he says : " If football is to be shorn of its vigour how are we to get that all-in action which the public demands."

He is consistent both in his play and in his policy and beliefs.

There are footballers who act unnaturally when they change their club colours for the colours of their country.

That cannot be said of Trevor Ford—watering down his approach would not be in character with the man, whatever the occasion.

There is nothing tepid either about the player or about the terraces' opinion of him. They are violently for him or just as violently against him.

As with men at the top in other walks of life, there can be no half-measures. And I fancy that is the way Ford would like it to be.

For my own part, I can only hope that the game will long benefit from the fire and vitality given it by this Red Dragon from Paradise Park.

TREVOR FORD (right) in play during this season's Sunderland v. Chelsea match

AN OLD-TIME 'CAP' FLAILS MODERN SOCCER

● ARTHUR BRIDGETT, who wrote this indictment of modern players and training methods, was the Sunderland and England outside-left from 1905 until 1914. He then became player-manager with South Shields until the early '20s, and now lives in Stoke. Two of his sons play for Stoke as amateurs.

HE SAYS IT'S PART OF THEIR PUNISHMENT TO WATCH THIS LOT

WHEN I read Billy Wedlock's article in "Football Monthly" a few weeks ago, it brought back to my mind the best exhibition of centre-half play I ever saw.

I happened to be the reserve for the Professionals' team when they met the Amateurs on Sheffield Wednesday's ground at Owlerton, in 1905. It was Wedlock who gave the wonderful display.

He arrived, after a hurried journey from Bristol, fully stripped for the match. Despite a tiring journey, he was here, there and everywhere the ball was. His energy was terrific.

After such a display he could not be left out of the England team. In fact, he was the centre-half for the next eighteen consecutive internationals.

Yet a young lad, Charlie Roberts, of Manchester United, was considered by the players of that day to be the best in the position.

Wedlock was the type that dominated the game in the days before the "stopper" centre-half was introduced. He was, from what I can gather, pretty similar to the Austrian centre-half, Ocwirk, who put up such a grand show against England at Wembley.

Why we cannot return to-day to the old-time attacking centre-half is beyond my comprehension. I can see no reason why a centre-half should be glued to his penalty-area.

Mention of the Austrians reminds me that I was one of the England party that made the first trip to Austria, in 1908.

They made a big fuss of the amateur, Vivian Woodward, and were well versed in the form of the rest of the team.

Yet we had substantial and easy victories in all games on that Continental trip except one, against Bohemia in Prague. They had previously beaten Manchester City, and no doubt, hoped to do the same with us.

Fortunately we got them to agree to have an English referee, Mr. John Lewis—afterwards an honoured member of the F.A.—and we won 4—0.

After the game, the crowd were so annoyed at the result that we had to be escorted to the pavilion.

When we eventually went out to the brakes awaiting to take us to the hotel, a hostile crowd was waiting. Ben Warren, our right-half, and a ninety-minutes hard player, took a bottle out with him and remarked: "The first one to interfere will get this."

It seems to me that the physique of modern players does not compare with that of the men of my days.

I can remember the Sunderland team of 1902-03—my first season with the club—when we were in the running for the First Division championship. We lost on the last day because of a 1—0 defeat at Newcastle.

We were taken to Seaton Carew for special training, and one day went to the Turkish baths at West Hartlepool. The masseur there was a physical culturist and had bar-bells up to 112lb.

The boys had a try at the heaviest, and four of the forwards, as well as myself, could put the 112lb. bar above their heads with one hand.

The forwards were Billy Hogg, 13st. 7lb.; Mark Watkins, 12st. 7lb.; Alf Common, 13st.; Jimmy Gemmell, 14st. 7lb; and myself, 13st.

Can you imagine a team turning out to-day with a front line as big as that! They would cause a sensation.

One thing particularly impresses me about the modern play—the poor shooting of most forwards. That I put down mainly to training methods.

In the old days we used to devote at least one day a week to shooting practice. It brought results.

Playing for Time . . .

EACH day, manager Tom Whittaker's desk at Arsenal is piled with letters. Some are from boys who want trials, some from old players who retain the Arsenal "family" feeling and like to keep in touch . . .

Look through that mail, and you find many odd requests, but none quite so strange as one which was addressed to "The Arsenal Football Association, England." From an earnest footballer in the Belgian Congo it asked:

1. Does penalty follow after three consecutive corners?
2. Any way of attack shoulder against shoulder with the purpose to displace the rival and take away from him the ball. Is it to be considered as foul?
3. Involuntary hands. Is it to be considered as such?
4. In case of foul, but the rival continues to advance with ball—is it any usefulness to take it as such?
5. I am just in front of goal, ready to shoot. Time is just over. The referee, has he the right to whistle before I shoot? And if I shoot and score goal, has he the right to cancel it?
6. Has the referee the right to order any player to get outside the ground before drawing his attention and without any notice to the captain?

CROSSWORD SOLUTION

ACROSS: 1, Matchless; 8, Unequal; 9, Rotherham; 11, Milburn; 14, Everton; 15, Oread; 16, Rowe; 18, Soho; 19, Kelso; 20, Wand; 23, Name; 26, Price; 29, Odds; 30, Date; 33, Crags; 35, Prairie; 36, Ascetic; 37, Headaches; 38, Endorse; 39, Doncaster.

DOWN: 1, Mortensen; 2, Tottenham; 3, Enhance; 4, Summers; 5, Yellow; 6, Queue; 7, Bland; 10, Eats; 12, Brew; 13, Rain; 17, Ooze; 19, Kept; 21, Aldershot; 22, Dispenser; 24, Airs; 25, Edge; 27, Reached; 28, Captain; 31, Astern; 32, Gala; 33, Capel; 34, Acids.

All hands to the deck for the Sunderland defence at Stamford Bridge.

Threadgold the Sunderland goalkeeper watches this Arsenal shot go narrowly wide.

Trevor Ford in action against Newcastle.

★ACTION★

Trautmann the Manchester City keeper pounces to foil Trevor Ford of Sunderland.

More action from the Manchester game, as Len Shackleton screws his shot wide of the goal.

Keep These "Reforming" Meddlers out of Football

WHITHER are we going ? That phrase is my constant companion, and the more I read and discuss football with divers people, the more I am certain the answer is not forthcoming.

One bright and sunny day someone will awaken and discover that football is a game and go into sackcloth and ashes over the loss of reams of paper, gallons of ink and years in hours which have been utterly wasted on the bilge written about the sport.

For nearly thirty-two years football has been my bread and butter—or was it margarine when I was playing ?

On reflection, the thought is encouraged that, with certain reservations, I am qualified to say a few words on the game.

When I think of the twenty seasons downstairs the words of Isaac Watts come readily to my mind :—

" *I have been there and still would go,*
 'Tis like a little heaven below."

So all ye aspirants to the sanctum with " Boss " on the door, take heed !

It is natural that, when one has been wrapped up in football for so long, one should take a very keen interest in its welfare.

To me, football is in a parlous state through no fault of its own, but through the machinations of a certain set with misguided conceptions of the game—men who refuse to leave well alone.

The biggest crime against the game was committed in 1925 when the off-side rule was altered and the punishment was made to fit the crime—the stopper centre-half for life.

From then we have had the reformers roaming at large with their novel ideas—two referees, goal-line judges, extending the penalty line, etc.

And those of us who love the game find solace in the fact that the path of a reformer is a thorny one, and that none of those " reforms " came to pass.

The off-side rule, however, *was* altered, to assist the brainless forwards who could not obey the fundamental principle of keeping behind the ball.

Now the latest stunt is to prevent the full-back passing the ball back to his goalkeeper.

The full-back who takes a risk, I admit, makes for more spectacular and entertaining football but, unlike forwards who are remembered for their successes, he is remembered for his mistakes, so his maxim should be—" take no risks."

In my opinion, stopping a full-back passing back is tantamount to asking him to disregard another principle of good football—that of playing the way you are looking.

Throughout the years we have had memorable games in the epic category. If the game was not good enough, as it was, then those epics could not have taken place—so to those who don't like the game I say, " Please stop messing it about."

Fundamentally, the game is the same to-day as it was sixty years ago. For that we owe eternal thanks to the far-seeing legislators who framed the rules and regulations when the League was formed.

Yet while, basically, the game is the same, there is a difference. There is more finesse. It is more streamlined —as befits the modern trend.

Gone is the good old-fashioned shoulder charge, for which I personally mourn—the fun, the excitement of pitting one's physical strength against another has to be experienced to be believed.

It made one feel good to be alive, yes, and believe it or not players earned the healthy respect of each other.

There is not enough football played just for the fun of it, the type of football which produced the natural player, not the robot who is the product of an over-coaching system, in which players are lectured to satiation point on tactics until they are " blinded by their own science."

I say : Give them a respite from the carefully-ordered, made-to-plan football and give the natural player a chance to develop.

What produced the Buchans, Mordues, Penningtons, Seeds, Jacks and Jameses and their contemporaries ?

Certainly it was not the lecture room. No, they graduated through the school of experience.

Charles Buchan in an earlier issue of this magazine, tells the story of how Montgomery, of Notts County.

WHERE ARE TO-DAY'S DAVID JACKS ?

taught him in one sharp lesson not to try to beat an opponent twice-running with the same trick. Please note—*one* lesson.

In the school of experience there is no gown and mortar-board ; the Queen's English may be conspicuous by its absence, but nevertheless, this school turned out more "Honours" pupils than any modern school.

Don't misunderstand me, I am not against coaching altogether, but this coaching, from the primary school age to the provident scheme age, will produce only quantity—not quality.

Are we trying to be too clever in turning football into a science, with all this streamlining and finesse ?

From finesse it is but a short step to largess which brings us to the most controversial point in football.

I should say there is more bilge said and written on soccer finance than on any other football matter by people who ought to have more sense.

It would be all so simple if everyone realised that football is a game, not a business . . .

If it was business, then tradition, sentiment, and all the things that make football what it is would have to go overboard. But we are not prepared to make that sacrifice (which I think is to our credit), so a happy medium must be found.

Football is unique in many respects—none more so than when money matters are introduced. It does not bear comparison with an ordinary business.

And that is where so many fall down. They attempt to apply ordinary business methods, which don't work.

I have discussed the financial angle with responsible officials, Press and players and I have the feeling the latter are being led unwittingly up the garden-path.

Too often, gross figures are quoted. Too often it is forgotten that no individual makes a profit out of a game, that any profit a club makes belongs to the club.

The share capital of most clubs is ridiculously small, with the interest limited to $7\frac{1}{2}$ per cent.

The clubs who have a healthy bank balance can use that money only for the benefit of the club, not for any individual or set of individuals.

The rich clubs are invariably quoted in support of the players' claims for an increase of wages, but the claims ignore the fact that the rules are framed not for the rich clubs alone, but for *all* clubs.

It is possible for a player to receive the maximum in a poor club just as in a rich club.

The wages are decided every year and so long as the rules are framed on the game as a whole the rich clubs cannot pay more than the rules permit.

I will always agree with, and defend the right of, every player to get as much as he can out of the game, if circumstances support him, but every player should realise he can take out only what he puts in.

Every player who signs a contract does so of his own free will. No one compels him. He should realise that a player's life is a precarious one, that he can do a humpty-dumpty act any day.

Through no fault of his own, illness, injury, loss of form can overtake him. But, if he does not take cognisance of these facts he will have a perpetual grouse against the conditions of the game.

No one will deny there is a lot of money in football, but it is not sufficient for a tithe of the grandiose schemes I have heard mooted.

I do, however, sincerely believe that there is more than enough to satisfy a reasonable wage increase and a fund for the support of seriously injured players and those stricken with illness.

I don't profess to be a Solomon, but what I would like to see is the inauguration of a small body of men with professional football in their veins, men born and brought up in the game, with no club connections and no axe to grind.

They should be given a job of solving our problems and keeping the game on an even keel.

They would be employed and paid through the game and it would be money well spent.

I certainly feel that asking clubs to make decisions of paramount importance, within an hour or two, at an annual meeting is asking too much.

JENKINS   Consulting the Linesman

ARTHUR WRIGHT

Sunderland

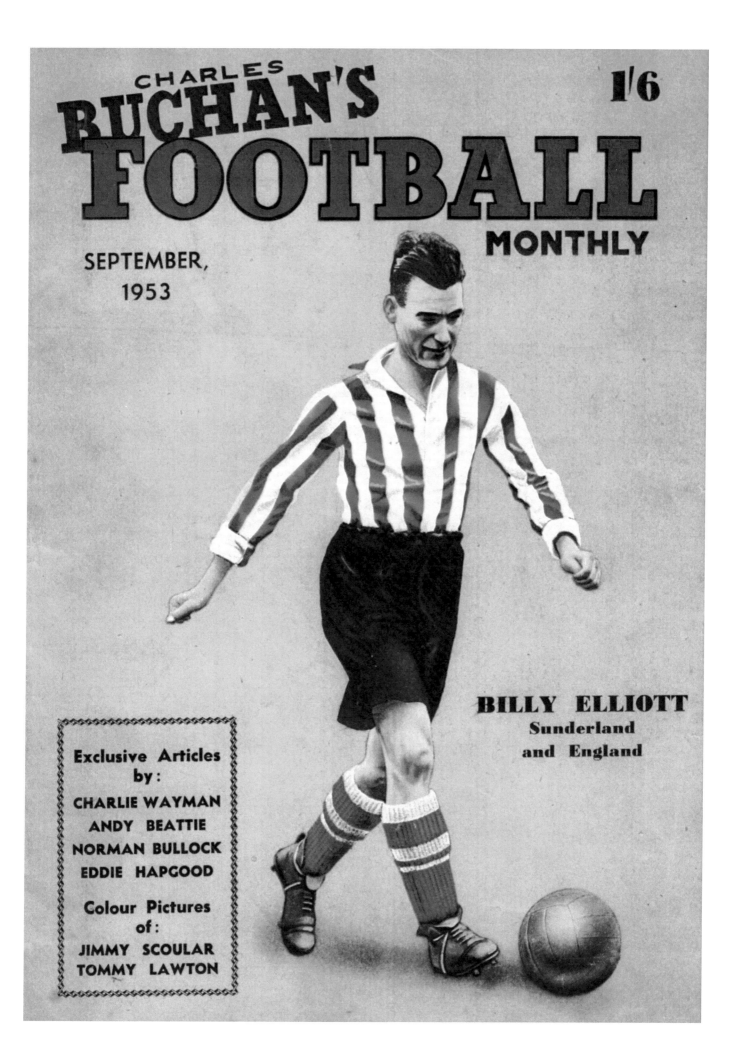

CHARLES
BUCHAN'S
FOOTBALL
MONTHLY

1/6

SEPTEMBER,
1953

BILLY ELLIOTT
Sunderland
and England

Exclusive Articles
by :
CHARLIE WAYMAN
ANDY BEATTIE
NORMAN BULLOCK
EDDIE HAPGOOD

Colour Pictures
of :
JIMMY SCOULAR
TOMMY LAWTON

YOU'VE GOT TO BE FIT!

"FIND 'em young!" is the slogan with all big football bosses—and there is a wealth of wisdom in the technique.

Men who make the big-time grade in the game are, without exception, players who possessed an in-born love of soccer almost from the moment they were old enough to kick a ball.

In my own case, from the age of nine years, nothing else mattered to me but football. And, to be truthful, at the present time this state of affairs still applies.

At the age of nine I started playing for the local school team at Swansea in the centre-half position.

By

TREVOR FORD
Sunderland and Wales
Centre Forward

Later, as an emergency measure, I played left-back at my senior school and played there for quite a while, even after schooling was over.

Much to the disgust of my parents, lessons were often neglected in order that I might have a game of football on a park near to my home.

The first disappointment occurred at 13, when I was picked to play for Wales as a Schoolboy International and missed this "cap" by reason of a broken leg. Even today, on looking back, the loss of that "cap" remains a great disappointment.

AS soon as I was 17, I signed for Swansea Town as a left-back but, very soon after the outbreak of war, I was called up for Army service and there I was converted into a centre-forward which, on my return to "civvy street," continued to be my position.

Subsequently, as a centre-forward I have earned many caps for Wales, and hope to earn still more.

Joining up for service in H.M. Forces was certainly a great step in my career as, not only did I put on weight and height, both of which were badly needed, but it also enabled me to find my best position.

And this is one important lesson I should like to emphasise to the up-and-coming youngster. As speedily as possible, find out the position for which you think you are best suited and continue to play in that position.

It is very desirable, and at times necessary, that a player should have versatility; but, with due respect to everyone concerned, I voice the opinion that there is one position, and one position only, in which an individual can give of his best.

He might be a good player in another position, but not so good as in the position which he himself favours.

I shall always subscribe to the opinion that a player is the best judge of the position to which he is most ideally suited.

AGAIN, like every other profession, hours of practice and concentration are necessary, and the value of "two-footedness" is too apparent to need emphasis.

Hours of practice are needed, and the two-footed player has the advantage every time over an opponent who can use only one foot. It is, indeed, surprising that in present day football there are a considerable number of players who rely on one foot for 90 per cent of the play.

Heading practice is another essential for all players. Particularly is this so in the case of forwards, as the

One of the best pictures of all time is provided by this graphic study of Trevor Ford scoring his second goal for Wales against England at Wembley last season. England won 5-2.

deflection and direction of a headed ball invariably can beat a defence if properly executed.

In this connection, perhaps I might refer to such well-known forwards as Dixie Dean and Tommy Lawton, both masters at this phase of the game, but only by reason of the old adage—Practice makes perfect!

Bodily fitness is another essential, and pays off handsome dividends to the young player who will persevere in this direction and strive for maximum fitness all the year round.

I WOULD draw attention to my own position of centre-forward.

The centre-forward is the spearhead of the attack and is bound to give and take some hard knocks in his quest for goals.

The same thing, of course, applies to defenders. There is no mollycoddling on the football field, and no worth-while player expects to be mollycoddled.

One of football's most outstanding attractions is the fact that it is a "man's game." It is a healthy, full-blooded business. And always bear in mind that it is ninety minutes' action and goals that the public demands. To provide the customers with full value for money, a player must be 100 per cent fit.

There are, of course, various styles of play and some exponents of our great game are more robust than others.

My own style of action falls into the robust category and I rarely emerge from any game without a fair share of hard knocks and buffeting.

So—bodily fitness! I cannot too strongly stress its terrific importance.

MOST great players admit to kicking a ball whenever the opportunity offers and it is amazing what one can learn through daily practice, accompanied by a colleague, or even through taking out a ball solo and kicking it around.

And this brings me to another of my strong arguments.

A great deal of emphasis nowadays is placed upon

formance of speed with the ball at one's feet?

No doubt you have seen, or experienced for yourself, t h i s fallacy of speed. Suddenly a player puts on a great burst of speed, but by the time he reaches his objective he is no longer in possession of the ball. He was moving so fast he left the ball behind enroute!

As I say, anyone can run, and most chaps can work up a high degree of speed. But what is the use of that speed if you cannot control the ball at the same time?

★

IN short, my advice to youngsters who have a love for this great winter game of ours, is to find and stick to their best position; practice to become proficient with both feet as well as the head, and strive always for bodily fitness.

One m o r e point. Whenever the opportunity presents itself, model your play on the style of the leading players of the moment who occupy your chosen position. Endeavour always to emulate such players, and strive for the elusive perfection which, while always just around t h e corner,

"Most great players admit to kicking a ball whenever the opportunity offers; and it is amazing what one can learn through daily practice," says Ford.

speed off the mark. As a matter of fact I am inclined to the belief that this speed business is becoming rather over-done.

To my mind, we would probably see much better football than sometimes we do if youngsters were instructed to train with the ball and not without it.

What is the use of being able to run fast in practice and, on match days, not to be able to equal this per-

persistently remains just out of reach.

More important still. Put everything you have got into your game. And if at times you feel just a little bit discouraged, remember that countless other youngsters, who are big names today, trod this self-same road before you.

They overcame their difficulties—and so can you. Good luck!

" That's MY ball," WILLIE FRASER, of Sunderland, seems to be saying as he dives perilously between two pairs of boots.

by
HARRY
THREADGOLD
(Sunderland goalkeeper)

SOMETIMES people ask me to name the first essential of the goalkeeping art. Two or three answers spring to mind, but I am always prompted to emphasise the need for a good reach.

It may sound an obvious requirement for the man whose job it is to keep high and low balls out of the net ; I have had good reason to know just how vital it is.

Goalkeeping has always been my first love, in the positional sense. But I was very small as a boy and had to be agile and quick-thinking to neutralise my inability to reach the balls that were moving away from me.

Clear in my memory is a match at Ninian Park, Cardiff. I was playing for Chester Boys in the final of the Welsh Schools Shield.

★

IT was a great occasion for us and we were eager to win. But Cardiff Boys, our opponents, scored the only goal of the game with a high ball that was beyond my reach.

You don't forget things like that !

I refused to be discouraged by my shortness but I must give credit to the officials in charge of the Chester Boys' team. I was only 4ft. 10in., but that did not prejudice my selection.

I remember how small I felt in those days. Both my full-backs were 5ft. 10in., a foot taller than I !

When I was 15, I joined the Navy. The life on the ocean wave developed me physically and gave me the inches I had lacked as a boy.

My goalkeeping aspirations received a jolt in my early days in the Navy. I found myself in the company of some good players and the goalkeeper was too sound to be moved.

So I was given the inside-left position—and had to make the best of it.

Eventually, I got round to my

favourite position and I picked up some valuable experience in Naval football.

Once in Bombay, I was pitchforked into a representative team at the last minute, against the R.A.F. Guarding the other net was Ted Ditchburn, the Spurs' goalkeeper, and I remember how I watched him in admiration from the other end of the field.

★

MOST young footballers with ambition take the opportunity of studying the noted professional players who occupy their own positions on the field.

You can learn a lot that way, but in my own boyhood I chose to study closely a goalkeeper in the local Chester and District League.

He was just a local amateur at the time, but has since risen to Welsh international rank with Plymouth Argyle.

His name, if you haven't guessed it already, is Bill Shortt.

I followed Bill's footsteps by playing in the Chester and District League. I gained a place in the first team of the local Tarvin club and, after five games with them, was signed by Mr. Frank Brown, the Chester manager, on amateur forms.

Then came a run with the reserve team in a Cheshire League match at Macclesfield, during the local Wakes Week. I turned professional a few days later.

Chester's senior goalkeepers at that time were George Scales and Jimmy McLaren. Jimmy moved to Carlisle

ME A FORWARD!

United on a free transfer, but the club filled the gap by signing Ted Elliot, from Wolves.

A series of injuries hampered my progress about that time, but I was given my chance in the League team when Elliot was unfit, two seasons ago.

MY transfer from Chester to Sunderland last summer enabled me to fulfil a double ambition. I always wanted to play on Arsenal's ground at Highbury, and against Joe Mercer, their famous skipper, who also comes from Cheshire, and is something of an idol in that part of the country.

My wish was gratified in our second match this season, and it proved quite a day. Our 2—1 victory was Sunderland's first over Arsenal at Highbury for twenty-one years.

Bill Murray, our manager, was delighted. He had played in Sunderland's previous Highbury win in 1931, and was anxious to break the club's run of failure on Arsenal's field.

Needless to say, it was a happy occasion for me, playing in my first away game for the club.

That match was only my second in London. Last season I played for Chester in the third round cup-tie in which we held Chelsea to a draw at Stamford Bridge, but the Highbury crowd of 58,000 was the biggest I had faced.

It's a big jump from Third to First Division football, and the vastness of the crowds and spaciousness of the grounds make a big contrast with those in the Northern Section of Division Three.

I SHALL never forget the deep impression made on me by the imposing lay-out of Sunderland's ground at Roker Park when I arrived from Chester.

Mr. Murray showed me round and I quickly sensed that I had linked up with one of the finest clubs in football.

Here's a tip that may help budding young goalkeepers.

When at Chester, Bernard Port and I used to stage our own training session. I would stand four yards from a wall with Bernard, who was Chester's other goalkeeper, a few yards behind me. While I faced the wall, he would throw the ball against it to give me practice at stopping the rebound.

Back would come the ball at unexpected angles, and by taking turns at throwing it, we were able to give each other much valuable practice.

When boys ask my advice about goalkeeping I always stress as strongly as I can the importance of practice.

I expect most goalkeepers would say the same. Only by constant practice is it possible to improve your anticipation, agility and " goal-mouth sense."

Stunts such as we tried at Chester remove all monotony from training sessions because of their novelty. I know I always enjoyed them tremendously.

And mention of goalkeeping practice takes me back again to my schooldays. There was an orchard near my home, and a couple of trees were perfectly placed to form goal posts.

A friend and I made capital use of nature's work by using the trees for kicking in. There was just one snag. At harvest time, a hefty shot against one of the trunks would bring a cascade of fruit down on my head !

Harry Threadgold.

 ## SUNDERLAND'S CUP WIN

GREAT events turn on little things. A simple flick or nod of the head and a Soccer game can change completely.

A typical case was the Sunderland and Preston North End F.A. Cup Final, at Wembley, in April, 1937. And the man whose head touch transformed the situation was Bob Gurney, Sunderland's Durham-born, bustling centre-forward.

At half-time Preston were leading by a goal scored by centre-forward Frank O'Donnell. The outlook did not look too promising for Sunderland when North End started the second half full of confidence, all out to clinch the issue with a second goal.

Then Sunderland broke away and forced a corner on the left-wing. The ball sailed into the goalmouth and Gurney made a frantic effort to head through. Goalkeeper Mick Burns got to the ball first and punched it away.

As Gurney walked away with his back to the goal, the ball was returned quickly. The centre-forward jerked the back of his head to it and it sailed into the net.

There was a loud cry for offside. Gurney was no more than three yards from the goal when he deflected the ball, but referee R. G. Rudd had noticed one important fact that most of the on-lookers had not seen.

Andy Beattie, Preston left-back, was standing with his hand resting against the post, the position he had taken up for the corner-kick.

So quickly had the event happened, that he had had no time to move.

That equalising goal was the turning point of the game. From that moment Sunderland took command. When Raich Carter, international inside-right, put on a second goal, there was little doubt about the result, but outside-left Eddie Burbanks emphasised Sunderland's superiority with a third goal.

It was the first time Sunderland had won the F.A. Cup in their long and distinguished history. A lot of the credit for the triumph went to Gurney.

He was more than a centre-forward at that time. He was the inspiration of the attack, the man who ceaselessly worried the opposing defenders and gave his inside forwards, Carter and " Paddy " Gallacher, the time and scope to show their craft.

Out on the wings one moment, in the goalmouth the next, Gurney was never idle. He was the link in one of the greatest forward lines ever—Duns, Carter, Gurney, Gallacher, Burbanks.

He played no small part in Sunderland's peak period, seasons 1935-36 and 1936-37, when they won the First Division championship and the F.A. Cup in successive seasons.

Though he played only once for England—against Scotland, in 1935—Gurney was an invaluable asset to Sunderland for many years.

It was his one club. From the time he joined them from Bishop Auckland in the mid-twenties, until the day he retired from active service at the start of the war, his one home was Roker Park.

He was discovered when Sunderland played Bishop Auckland in a charity match at Darlington. Gurney scored two goals for the amateurs and Sunderland were not satisfied until he joined them.

He had the happy knack of being able to get goals when they were most needed. Sunderland's attack never moved with the same rhythm without him.

Gurney's style brought many hard knocks and injuries. But he was always the fearless raider, respected by opponents ; a team-man if ever there was one.

After a preliminary spell in charge of Peterborough United, the Southern League club, Gurney is now manager of the keen Darlington side. He will work his way to the top flight.

JIMMY COWAN

Sunderland and

Scotland

Off the field at Sunderland

First, there are autographs to be signed. Billy Elliott and Len Shackleton are surrounded by a crowd of young admirers.

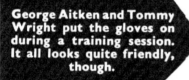

George Aitken and Tommy Wright put the gloves on during a training session. It all looks quite friendly, though.

After training is over a drink of pop is always welcome. (Left to right) are Shackleton, Bingham, Stelling and A. Wright.

GEORGE AITKEN

Sunderland and Scotland

tells how he crossed the Border to join the English club

A policeman called in the middle of the night

HAVE you ever been awakened by a knock on the front door in the middle of the night ? If you have, you'll understand what a shock it was when I saw the shadowy form of a policeman after groping my way downstairs.

His message was urgent, but there was no cause for alarm.

I was a Third Lanark player at the time, and Alex Ritchie, the club manager, had used this extreme measure to tell me to meet him at a Glasgow hotel the next morning.

That was all the policeman could tell me, and I returned to bed wondering what was afoot.

Although I was playing for Thirds, I was living at home, in Lochgelly, and training on the Raith Rovers' ground at Kirkcaldy.

It was in the early hours of a Friday morning that the message reached me, and at 12 o'clock, at the Glasgow rendezvous, I was told what it was all about.

There, with Mr. Ritchie, was Bill Murray, the Sunderland manager, and his mission was my signature to transfer forms.

I had been with Third Lanark less than a year, so Sunderland's interest was a great surprise.

No pressure was put on me. I was asked if I would like to join Sunderland, but, as Third Lanark were short of cash, they could not afford to discourage Mr. Murray's interest.

I discussed the matter over lunch with Mr. Murray, and as the idea sank in, the more I liked it.

He pointed out that I would find plenty of fellow-Scots at Roker Park, and as I knew Tommy Wright, the Sunderland outside-right—from his Partick Thistle days—I knew I would soon feel at home.

To cross the border to play for Sunderland, one of the greatest of England's clubs, was an exciting prospect. I signed the forms right away.

Then came the next surprise : " Can you pick up your boots and travel to

Sunderland as quickly as possible ? " asked Mr. Murray. " I want to play you against Fulham at Sunderland tomorrow."

That meant a dash over to Cathkin Park, Third Lanark's ground, to get my football boots, and then a hustle back home to Lochgelly to break the news to the family.

I left home that night for Edinburgh, and there caught the night train to Newcastle. I arrived in the small hours of the morning, but Sunderland had booked a room for me in the Station Hotel.

After breakfast next morning Mr. Murray called to take me to Sunderland.

I had spent much of the night sitting up in the train and had not had the best preparation for my first game in English football.

We drew the game 2—2, and frankly, I don't think I played too well.

That was the start of my association with Sunderland, and I can honestly say that I have never regretted taking the plunge into English football.

There was a time, I know, when Scots were coming across the border into English football in a seemingly endless stream. It's not like that now.

I believe this to be due, to some extent, to the fact that part-time professionalism, now prevalent in Scottish football, enables a player to earn a double wage that exceeds the maximum Soccer pay in England.

And on top of that, he has, of course, a job that

secures his future when Soccer days end.

But a player who is determined to reach the top has a better chance in England.

Full-time professionalism means full-time training, and maximum fitness is the result.

Nothing is more important to a footballer than regular training and the ability to last the ninety minutes.

I know from hard experience. At the time of my transfer from East Fife, my first club, to Third Lanark, in the middle of season 1950-51, I had been out of the game for a few months.

I had taken a job with a firm of contractors at Lochgelly and when I returned to football with Thirds, I went straight into their League side.

The match was at Aberdeen, and I survived the first half without feeling any undue strain.

But it was different in the second half. My lack of training began to tell, and it seemed as if my legs were made of lead.

I've told you how I made my entry into English football. The story of my Soccer beginnings goes back, however, to my early years in Lochgelly.

" I wish someone would hurry up and invent permutations!"

" Travel to Sunderland as quickly as possible " said Bill Murray, the Sunderland manager.

" My first match for Third Lanark as a centre-half was against Laurie Reilly " (above).

Willie Cunningham, of Preston, a colleague of Aitken in the Cowdenbeath and District team.

" I asked Major Frank Buckley (above) to cancel my amateur registration with the Wolves."

Like most players, I started to kick a ball when very young. I was only about ten when I began playing at left-back for Lochgelly South School.

Lochgelly is a small mining village, and in front of a row of miners' houses, there was a patch of waste ground.

On that rough pitch we practised hour after hour, and staged a gala session each Sunday. We pooled our pennies to buy a rubber ball. Sometimes it was nine-a-side—sometimes fewer.

It was football in its crudest form, but it was the best way to master the fundamentals of the game.

When I was eleven I was switched to the Lochgelly East School. Fortunately, what little reputation I had at that time must have preceded me.

I went into the school team as a centre-half, and now came within the range of selection for the Cowdenbeath and District team.

I managed to get into this local representative side. In it with me were Jimmy Baxter and Willie Cunningham, who are now stars of Preston North End.

Jimmy played at inside-forward and Willie at full-back, the positions they still occupy in League football.

The height of my achievement as a schoolboy was selection for an international trial at Kelty. I played in the game, full of hope and wild ambition, but was disappointed.

Selection for the schoolboys of Scotland was not for me.

At 14 I left school and went into the pits. I had no intention of neglecting my football and when I was 15½, I was playing for Bowhill West End, a club near Lochgelly, in secondary juvenile class.

My next move took me to Lochgelly St. Andrew's. It was while playing for that club in a juvenile league that I was spotted by Wolves.

A scout came to my home at Lochgelly. " Would you like to play for Wolves ? " he asked.

I was excited at the suggestion, but my father had died a few years previously, and I was not keen on leaving my widowed mother. I met him half-way by signing amateur forms.

But during the next month or two I decided that Wolverhampton was too far away from home.

So I wrote to Major Frank Buckley, the present Walsall manager, who was then in charge of Wolves, asking him to cancel my amateur registration.

Major Buckley agreed immediately, and thus ended my short association with Wolves.

During the time I was on their books, I never kicked a ball for them,

visited their ground or set foot in Wolverhampton.

Things happened quickly after that. Peter McLean, a friend of mine in Lochgelly, had signed for East Fife, and his father was keeping a look-out for talent for the Methil club.

Knowing my registration with Wolves had been cancelled, Mr. McLean approached me on behalf of East Fife.

I agreed to play a trial, but you can imagine my surprise when I heard that it was to be in East Fife's first team, against Dunfermline.

My feelings were not improved when I learned I was to take the place at centre-half of John Sneddon, who was injured.

Sneddon had played in East Fife's Cup-winning team of 1938, and I knew my inexperience would show up when deputising for such a noted player.

I managed to " get by " in that game, however, and when Sneddon returned for the following match, I was switched to right-half.

I kept my place in the team in that position, and most of my professional career has been spent in the wing-half berth.

Sunderland have played me at centre-half on occasions, and I have played a few games in that position for Third Lanark.

My first match at centre-half for Thirds was in opposition to Laurie Reilly, of Hibernian . . . and in the next game I had to face Willie Bauld, of Hearts.

What a test for an emergency centre-half ! Reilly and Bauld are two of the finest centre-forwards in the game.

As a left-half, I have a particular interest in inside-rights. I've met some brilliant players in that position, but if I had to nominate the greatest I have opposed, my vote would go to Wilf Mannion, of Middlesbrough.

When Wilf decided to quit football last summer, the game lost one of its greatest exponents.

But it's an ill wind that blows nobody any good . . . his retirement has spared Second Division left-halves a lot of headaches this season !

A BALL ARTIST HITS OUT

"How can any of our coaching ideas possibly succeed if the chaps doing the coaching are not 100% masters of ball control?"

Make England coaches pass MY test

says LEN SHACKLETON, Sunderland and England

THERE are big things wrong with big football in England, and when Charles Buchan invited me to air my views in " Football Monthly " on this highly topical subject I was, quite frankly, delighted.

Our international teams have been severely criticised for the poor results obtained from recent games, and as an active participant in big-time Soccer it is perhaps only natural that I should take up my pen on behalf of that much-maligned character, the player.

I have in mind those two games last May, against Yugoslavia and Hungary.

Now, to be quite fair, it must be remembered that our lads had just completed a season, most of them having figured in 40 or 50 League and Cup games. And, from experience, I can tell you that by the time a player has operated throughout such a full programme he has had sufficient football for a month or so and is ready for a rest.

Granted, once upon a time our League clubs could go abroad after a hard season at home, play against Continental clubs and even international teams, and win quite easily. But times have changed.

The Continentals are just learning the game, compared to the time it has been an organised business with us. They have proved apt pupils, and we now have to face the grim fact that, whereas they play the game *properly*, we don't.

Look at the Hungarians. Their players have the ability to control a ball perfectly. They can " kill " it stone-dead in an instant or, if the needs be, pass it very accurately first time to a team-mate.

Every man throughout the team is master of the ball. Which is more than you can ever say of any current England team. And that, I am firmly convinced, is where England's international headache begins.

Quite candidly I have little faith in our coaching system.

We have developed a big coaching scheme, quite a costly business (provided largely, may I add, by professional football). Therefore, to criticise the system is quite a serious matter. But there you are ; I am pulling no punches.

In the first place I will ask a very simple question. How can any of our coaching ideas possibly succeed if the chaps doing the coaching are not 100 per cent. masters of ball control ?

No man has the right to be coaching young boys (our future internationals) if he is not master of the subject which he is called upon to impart. And that, believe me, is the state we are in at present.

Mastery of the ball is the be-all and end-all of football. It is useless to drag out the blackboard with all sorts of phoney ideas on the game if you haven't first of all mastered the centre of attraction—the ball.

Maybe it's an easy thing to claim " I'd tell you what I would do." But give me control of this coaching

LEN SHACKLETON . . . is here almost submerged by a surge of boyish admirers.

system of ours and one of the first things I'd do would be to make all the so-called qualified F.A. coaches take a test in ball control. Those who failed to pass the test would come straight off the list.

Believe you me, if we are to regain our rightful place as the premier Soccer nation we must do this.

Unfortunately, to quote the greatest coach of them all, Jimmy Hogan (he taught the Hungarians), our Soccer is becoming the wrong type of " B's."

Jimmy says football is, above all, both " B's "—Brains and Ball Control, and not Bash and Boot.

The more I consider it, the more I realise that our Sunderland boss, Bill Murray, isn't talking through his hat, as so many people imagine, when he says our only salvation is to suspend the " bashing " for points in our League programme for at least one season and concentrate on letting our younger players learn to play the game the proper way—the Hungarian way, if you like.

This instead of throwing them into the fray as incomplete masters of their trade.

By this drastic action we could make up the ground we have lost to the Continentals. And, so far as I can see, it is the only chance we have.

The Continentals served their apprenticeship without the distraction —nay, wear and tear—of League and Cup hurly-burly such as ours. That, believe me, is how they have to-day become our masters.

The future alone will, of course, tell whether they eventually suffer our own experience and go in for the big business of league " warfare " and find themselves unable to replace star players by fully trained youngsters.

But we are not concerned with the future of the Continentals. It's England's future that matters, and we must not forget that it is the present that takes care of the future.

BILLY ELLIOTT
Sunderland and England

My side of the argument

By RAY DANIEL
Sunderland and Wales centre-half

LIKE life, football is full of contrasts. You find the men for whom everything seems to go right . . . and the luckless ones. You find the youngster just setting out on his chosen career . . . raw and unskilled . . . and you find the man of experience mastering his job.

And of all the contrasts that come to my mind as I reflect on my own career, the most marked is the one that arose during this season when I returned to Cardiff's Ninian Park as my country's centre-half.

For it was at this ground that I began my life as a professional footballer.

Looking back on myself in those days, I see a raw kid in his teens playing right-back for Swansea Town—and doing his best to make up for his lamentable rawness with any amount of enthusiasm.

Although I still have much to learn, my return to Cardiff was made under very different circumstances, for it was my thirteenth game for Wales, and apart from the change in position—from right-back to centre-half—my enthusiasm was now allied to a certain amount of skill and experience.

Whenever I reflect on that personal contrast, I am grateful to fortune for the chances it has given me. Apart from my Welsh caps, I have had the luck to land a League championship medal and a Cup Final runners-up medal, both awarded during my service with the Arsenal.

There has been, too, the publicity which attended my transfer, last June, to Sunderland, for a fee estimated at £30,000—a record for a man in one of the defensive positions of the field.

Yet all this has happened in a short time . . . it is only my third season in first-class football ! No wonder I am the first to admit that the breaks have come my way !

Since going to Sunderland, I have often been asked how I felt about the move, how playing for a town in a provincial centre compares with playing for a metropolitan club like Arsenal.

Perhaps the most remarkable feature that has struck me has been the keenness of the North-Eastern supporters. They are certainly more demonstrative than those in London. Everywhere in Sunderland there is one main topic of conversation—football !

Perhaps this may be more pronounced this season because of the opinions aroused by Sunderland's huge financial outlay for players during the close-season.

Besides myself they bought Jimmy Cowan, from Morton, and Billy Elliott, from Burnley. I am told that this brought the value of the team to the region of at least £150,000 !

It would be only natural to think that a team so expensively got together —with nine internationals studding it —would immediately carry all before it.

Unfortunately, the game does not work out like that at all. Players take time to settle down and to become accustomed to each other's play.

I am a firm believer in a centre-half being a constructive player, as well as a destructive one. I argue that football should be played right from your own goalmouth. . . .

I have been criticised by many people in the past for my own style of play. They say that I take too many chances, that by making a mistake I could give away a goal.

All I can say in response to my critics is that the results over the last two seasons I was with Arsenal justified the risk.

We reached Wembley two years ago, and finished third in the First Division, being beaten for second place on goal average. Last season we won the championship . . . not a bad record by any standards.

Now let us study the picture at Sunderland, as it was in the early part of the present season.

I found at first that the sort of football I was playing was in direct contrast to that of the other defenders around me.

The short pass that I was using was catching them unawares and consequently, we all were getting into trouble.

It inevitably takes time to find an understanding. Once again I am sure that satisfactory results will follow.

Another question I am asked is : " Do you regard football as a worthwhile career ? " **Without any doubt in my mind I answer that it is.**

Take my own case as an example. I do a job which I enjoy. My wife and I have a lovely home. We live comfortably, and within reason, I don't think we want for anything.

What of the insecurity of the game ? Well, I am starting a job beside Soccer, and I hope that this will give me a living when my time comes to hang up my boots.

A player on top money can earn £15 a week in the winter and £12 a week in the summer. There is also the £1 a point match bonus.

Besides this, a club can give a player a benefit of £750 after five years' service —which works out at another £3 a week.

★

Then if you are fortunate enough to play for your country there is another £50 for each game. And at the end of your career you get ten per cent. of all your earnings from football.

This means that after, say, twelve years in the game, a handsome sum has accumulated.

Quite apart from the financial side, there are other points which make the game worth-while.

In the past few years, for instance, I have been to South America, Portugal, Belgium, France, Yugoslavia and Switzerland, meeting people, seeing the sights and enjoying good company.

But for football, those faraway places would have been just names on the map to me.

Yet this great game is not all glitter. Don't forget that for every lad who reaches the top there are many who, for one reason or another, fail to graduate beyond second or third team status.

For them there are none of the rewards which I have described.

Yes, there are luckless ones in my job as there are in yours.

To any youngster contemplating a Soccer career I would say : " If you have the ambition and the determina-

Sunderland F.C. : Standing—Daniel, Hudgell, Watson, Cowan, Stelling, Aitken.
Sitting—Kirtley, Wright, Ford (now of Cardiff), Sheppeard, Elliott.

tion, and, of course, the ability, then football can be a very happy and exciting life.

" Be prepared to take the jeers as well as the cheers because at some time or another everyone of us gets a share of each."

It has given me many wonderful memories. Ranking highest among them all, to my mind, was Arsenal's Cup Final against Newcastle United two seasons ago.

For the beginning of that story we must go back to the Good Friday of that year . . . three weeks before Wembley.

Arsenal were playing at Blackpool. In the first minute, Stan Mortensen and I jumped for a high ball. The next thing I knew was that we were both lying on the ground a few feet from each other.

I realised immediately that my arm was broken, and my first frantic thought was that I would miss the Cup Final.

" No . . . there's no mistake, old boy . . . I am the Wolves' trainer."

The period that followed was full of worry, but after the bone had been set I did my training with my arm in plaster, and the anxious days sped by.

A few days before the big day the cast was taken off and a light, plastic one put on. That is how I played.

All went well until the tenth minute when I caught the damaged arm a terrific crack on something. I knew the bone had gone again !

I could feel a little pain, but the occasion was so exciting that I hardly noticed it.

There was no question of my not finishing the full ninety minutes, but the following week I had to go into hospital to have the arm set again.

This time the doctor's job was not as simple as in the first case, for the arm had taken a bad knock ; I had to have a silver plate inserted in the arm.

★

Perhaps that had something to do with my transfer value—silver is so valuable these days !

Stan Mortensen was also badly injured in that Good Friday collision.

He was unable to play for a long time, but it is typical of the Blackpool star's sportsmanship and generosity that he should have told me : " If you miss the Final I'll give you one of my medals."

What a wonderful gesture that was . . . and how typical of great-hearted Morty !

Yes, it is memories like this which *make* our national game—and men like Mortensen who do it credit. There are many like him, and I am grateful for their friendships.

And, as I concentrate on my greatest ambition—to help bring success to Sunderland—I look back on the game with sincere thanks for the happiness it has brought me. . . . *For, after all, it is happiness that we are all seeking.*

Firstly the action from the Valley where Charlton Athletic were the hosts.

'CAPITAL CAPERS' FOR SUNDERLAND

On to Stamford Bridge Chelsea, where the Wearsiders enjoyed better fortune.

"I walked to the ground . . . *it was raining* . . . I looked out of the window… *it was raining*…"

'Then I knew I was in England'

by TED PURDON

Sunderland

ONE Saturday afternoon soon after joining Birmingham City, I walked to the ground for a reserve match. It was pouring with rain as I entered the dressing room. For a time the players all chatted together, then the trainer said : " Come on, time to get changed."

A few started getting their kit ready. I moved to a window and looked out . . . it was still raining. I went back to my seat, certain the lads and the trainer were taking the " mickey " out of me.

But I soon realised it was no joke and that we were going to play—rain or no rain.

Then I knew I was in England—and I quickly met one of the big differences between football here and at home. Many other things surprised me, too—training for instance.

In South Africa our players are amateurs and they train in spare time. I was amazed to find here the remarkable organisation behind English League clubs, their planned programmes, coaches, technical equipment and medical rooms.

The speed of play and the brilliant heading ability were two other things very different from what I had previously encountered.

When I left Johannesburg the standard there was little better than in the English Third Division, but it was improving. This is borne out by the defeats of Newcastle United and Dundee, when on tour.

There is plenty of talent in South Africa, but it needs developing. I think the players who come to England, then return home, can make a big difference to their inexperienced countrymen.

Although I have no immediate intention of returning home I hope that when my career in the Football League is finished I'll be able to do so—and perhaps take up coaching.

Efforts are being made to introduce part-time professionals into South African football. If this succeeds it will be more difficult for British clubs to coax lads to come here because, by doing so, they would be worse off financially.

But, for players from my country really to learn the game, they have either to come here or be taught by coaches who have sampled your play.

It was as a centre-forward that I came to England having decided to join Birmingham—who had just been relegated—to gain experience, instead of signing for Blackpool with my old pal and rival Bill Perry.

My League debut, at Leeds, in September, 1951, was a great milestone because everything went well. I scored, and seemed set for a regular place.

However, I did not improve very quickly and it took all manager Bob Brocklebank's words to stop me going home despondent and sick of the sight of a football.

I stuck it out, battling with Bill Smith and Jimmy Higgins—back in Ireland—for a place at inside-forward, but it was only when I moved to centre-forward that I became really settled.

At the end of 1953 Birmingham told me Plymouth had made a big offer for my transfer, but having just married, and moved into a new house, I did not fancy the move.

A week later I changed my mind when I had a tip that Sunderland wanted me. When the rumours proved true I had no second thoughts about signing.

Birmingham seemed keen to let me go and the thought of joining such a famous First Division club was very flattering.

At the time, January, 1954, Sunderland were having a very poor run, but we won my first match 5—2 and I got two goals. In addition, I managed to help Len Shackleton to a goal, and, when this genius took a liking to me, it helped a lot.

The early success continued, and a week later I got the quickest-ever goal at Highbury. It was a ten-second affair in which I passed to Shack, who put the ball to Tommy Wright and I hit the centre home.

This started me on the way to my first hat-trick and a 4—1 victory.

We managed to clear relegation in just about the biggest possible blaze of publicity any League club could have.

Sunderland had signed internationals Jimmy Cowan, Ray Daniel and Billy Elliott before the season started. Then they transferred Trevor Ford, and bought Ken Chisholm and me.

Everyone talked of the " glamour club," " million dollar team," the " fancy boys " . . . and I think some probably said " the big heads."

Let me say most forcibly that when I joined Sunderland I went to a happy club where there was never any suggestion of dressing-room trouble.

The players did get a bit upset at times about our nicknames, but we got over that, helped by Ken Chisholm. He talked so fast and so much that no one had any time to worry.

Now we use the names ourselves . . . and they provide plenty of laughs for a grand bunch of lads.

" Hope you don't mind. When he asked me my name I gave him yours ! "

Chisholm . . . . was transferred whenever the buying club wanted a goal-getter.

ALL THIS, AND TOO!

by KEN CHISHOLM
Sunderland

SEVEN clubs in eight years . . . there isn't another player in the game who can equal that. After leaving Queen's Park in 1946 my travels took me to Partick, Leeds, Leicester, Coventry, Cardiff, then to Sunderland in 1954.

Let me point out quickly that no club has bought me without having a purpose in mind. All except Cardiff wanted me to get quick goals and save them from relegation. The Welsh club also wanted goals—but for promotion. And once again I obliged.

I've met some remarkable people in my wanderings—Marilyn Monroe, Joe Baksi, and Major Frank Buckley among them.

How comes a footballer to mix with the one and only Marilyn ? Well, it happened on Sunderland's 1955 tour of America.

We were given a daily allowance in New York and allowed to get meals wherever we wished. Invariably we ate at a restaurant about 50 yards from Broadway.

Next door were studios where the stars who were not making pictures spent their time at dramatic classes or having singing and dancing lessons.

Tuesday morning was Marilyn morning. Her lesson over she came in for lunch. Some of the lads thought her looks were not quite what they expected, but none of them was disappointed with her walk.

That is something, REALLY SOMETHING. I cannot describe it, it must be seen to be believed. But it really is dynamite.

Many other stars had meals at nearby tables, including Dane Clark, Patricia Neal and Shelley Winters.

Joe Baksi, who looked like one side of the Empire State Building, stopped us with a special message for Frank Swift. Apparently he had met the great goalkeeper while in England and sent good wishes to his pal.

Major Buckley came into my life when I joined Leeds United. He felt convinced I could win a place in Scotland's team—if I followed his training plan.

It meant " just a little hard work," he told me. Hard work ! It was positively a horrifying plan he suggested.

" Get up early and have a round of golf before breakfast," he said. " After a good meal come down here and do a morning's work at the ground. Go home for lunch, come back for afternoon training, then have a good tea followed by a long walk."

The final point was to be in bed by nine o'clock.

" Do that and I'll have you in the Scottish team in a month," he said.

My reply was quick. " You won't," I answered. " You'll have me in my grave."

We did not go ahead with this idea, but I must tell you how the Major improved my shooting.

He put a ball on the ground and huge bricks on either side. I had to run full tilt and smack the ball with my right foot as hard as possible. Oh, yes ! It improved my shooting. But, boy, what a mess it made of my nerves !

While talking of personalities I want to bring in Len Shackleton and Ray Daniel, colleagues at Sunderland.

One thing which interested me in a move to Sunderland was the thought of having Shack as the other inside-forward. I

CHISHOLM . . . when with Cardiff, leaps over goalkeeper Ditchburn, of Spurs.

MARILYN,

MARILYN MON-
ROE... "the
lads liked her
walk."

make no bones about my style. I'm there to get goals—he is the best fellow in the world for making them.

His methods may be unorthodox, but you can be certain that if you run into an open space the ball will eventually come—even though he may decide to send it by a back heel, or a flick over his head, or sometimes by a straightforward pass.

Before reaching Sunderland I was told he was a difficult customer, hard to get on with and full of tantrums. What nonsense that is ! Shack is a great character.

Daniel ? Well, you recall he got off to a bad start at Sunderland, but fortunately, the Welsh centre-half never lost his sense of humour.

" Bebe " has one special hobby—translating his large transfer fee into kroner, dollars or other foreign currency.

When we toured America he often spoke of his 87,000 dollar transfer fee. Not boastingly, but with impish fun.

What a turn they put on when he and Shack start on their fees ! Ray points out to Len how much more he cost. Len replies that comparison cannot be made.

" After all, mine took place when money was money. The pound has deteriorated since," he hits back.

I've had disappointments as well as good moments. Probably the biggest blow was when Leicester lost at Wembley to Wolves in 1949.

We went to the Cup Final without Don Revie who had done so much in earlier rounds.

At 1—2 down, the Leicester side suddenly clicked and Wolves did not know how to stop us. Stan Cullis was getting all worked up on the touchline as we took control.

Then I got away and scored. At least I thought I had when the referee pointed to the middle. It was the most wonderful moment of my life—until he walked to a flag-wagging linesman.

His decision was changed to off-side, the resultant free kick soared upfield and Sammy Smythe broke through and we were 1—3 down.

In a flash the course of the game had changed. We felt too despondent even to hope of getting a grip again.

A week later we had to get a point in the last game of the season, against Cardiff, to avoid relegation. Fifteen minutes from time we trailed 0—1 down, but we managed to pop one in for the vital point.

When I later joined Cardiff they had a fine defence, but needed someone to get goals for promotion. I played in only ten games but scored eight times. Cardiff won a First Division place on goal average, in 1952.

Invariably, I have got off to a good start at a new club. In my debut for Sunderland I scored an important goal.

Although they had so many stars the Roker club were in the middle of a bad run; never had I met such lack of confidence. But against Aston Villa I got the first goal after 20 minutes, and it seemed to help the team to relax and pull out their best.

SHELLEY WINTERS

JOE BAKSI

Average age of Ireland's attack is only 22. That should mean years of playing together—a good thing for us because . . .

FAMILIARITY BREEDS COMBINATION

says BILLY BINGHAM
Sunderland and Ireland

THE best thing to happen to Irish international football for many a day is that, at 23, I am "daddy" of the usual attack. I suppose that sounds rather "big-headed"—but it isn't meant to be.

It is simply an illustration to show forcibly the remarkably youthful forward line Ireland has been fielding.

My right-wing partner, Jackie Blanchflower, is 21. At centre-forward we have a 20-year-old, Billy McAdams; inside-left Jimmy McIlroy is 23, a couple of months my junior; at outside-left is 21-year-old Peter McParland.

That gives an average age of under 22. Barring accidents and loss of form we can expect a fair number of years together in the national side.

This is a vital point in Ireland's future team-building, for Hungary showed with their great team that blend can be achieved best by keeping a small number of players together as long as possible.

Already I find it is not difficult to anticipate the moves of Jackie, Billy, Jimmy or Peter. Not through telepathy—just familiarity.

I've heard it said that familiarity breeds contempt, but I find it brings combination.

The best example I ever had of the way in which knowledge of a colleague can help came in my first international match, against France, at Windsor Park, Belfast, in May, 1951.

Behind me in that debut, at right-half, was Danny Blanchflower. The last time I had been teamed with him was when we formed a right-wing triangle for Glentoran, with Jimmy McIlroy.

After a short time in that game with France I settled to Danny's passes as though there had been little break in our partnership.

In my next big match, against Scotland, I was able to link up with McIlroy, and

the trio was complete again when we faced Wales towards the end of the season.

Back to that game against France.

Opposing me was Roger Marche, a really first-class back. But, with Danny Blanchflower working fine openings, I was able to use my speed fully and have a good debut.

The biggest moment in the match was also a bitter disappointment. I beat the defence and put the ball past goalkeeper Da Rue while the fans roared. But all my glee disappeared when the "goal" was disallowed.

Some of my Irish colleagues consider that the turn in Ireland's fortunes did not come until later, but I am convinced that our 2—2 draw with France was the key game. It brought confidence—which was one of the things most needed in the team.

Probably my best international was against Scotland this season. The goal I scored, in another 2—2 draw, had a humorous twist.

One of my best friends at Sunderland is goalkeeper Willie Fraser. During this game he cleared the ball by throwing to a colleague.

I was standing behind this player, and, being much smaller, was hidden from Willie.

As the ball came out I rushed forward, breasted it down and smashed it past my pal.

"Not you . . . anyone but you," he groaned.

You can imagine the inquests we held when I visited him for a TV show the next day.

The impact Peter Doherty has made on the Irish side is obvious, and well known.

Credit must also go to

Gerry Morgan, our trainer. A cheerful dressing-room is a wonderful help—Gerry certainly sees we have that.

He seems to have a natural aptitude for making players happy and is always playing jokes on us.

Naturally, we play them on him . . . one of our most successful being the "cocktail" hoax which occurred before this season's match with England.

Before lunch in a luxury hotel near the Mountains of Mourne, Gerry was offered a delightful-looking "cocktail" from which he took a good mouthful.

What an explosion followed! We had filled the glass with vinegar, mustard, pepper and numerous other things.

Poor Gerry nearly blew the roof away . . . but a few minutes later was bellowing with laughter.

One of my great ambitions is to play at Wembley. Perhaps this will be achieved with Ireland.

We can honestly say we are now equal to any of the other teams in the international tournament. A Wembley date would be a grand gesture by England.

KEN CHISHOLM
Sunderland

"I have been called dirty," says **BILLY ELLIOTT**, *of Sunderland and England. "There have been wild stories about my transfers, rumours of jealousy at Roker Park. Here is my . . .*

REPLY TO THE CRITICS

"THERE are twenty-two players in a match and all have a share in the ball. But when you go into a tackle, forget about fair shares—come out with the ball all to yourself."

That advice was given to me by the best captain I have ever known—Bob Danskin, former Bradford centre-half.

Now, because I try to carry out that advice, I have been called dirty, robust, and rough.

I never intend to be any of these. I want the ball, yes, because I'm paid to get it. But I want it fair and square.

Danskin taught me never to squeal, to take and give hard knocks. And he also taught me the meaning of discipline.

Youngsters who get quickly spoilt in present-day football would not have liked the way our skipper handled beginners.

We spoke only when we were spoken to. If a youngster piped up out of turn the captain would fix him with a piercing stare.

The lad knew only too well to take it as a warning.

Often have I thought of that early training, and been thankful because it has allowed me to take the ups and downs—which come to all players—as part of the job.

Because I took part in two big transfers—totalling £53,000, I'm told—in a period of 21 months, there have been all sorts of wild stories.

So, for the first time, I now tell the background of those moves.

When Bradford were relegated (in 1950) to the Third Division, I asked for a transfer. I liked the club, and the players—and they had many good ones—but I was convinced a better future lay with a senior team.

However, I did not press the request, and eventually decided to have one full season in the Division to give it a full trial.

At the end of the season I was quite set on a move and refused to re-sign. I lost financially—but achieved my desire.

Wolves were first to make an offer, and Sunderland showed interest, but apparently would not meet Bradford's £23,000 fee.

Burnley then entered the bidding, and the short move across the county border suited me.

My brief time at Turf Moor was full of success. I found top form, really struck combination with Les Shannon—one of the most underrated players I have met—and seemed well settled.

Why then did I make another move? To end imaginative tales, here are the facts.

Before the 1953-4 season Burnley offered me sliding scale terms. Frankly, I thought them unfair and would not accept.

When asked to re-sign I would not do so. My old contract had not expired, and I wanted time to think things over.

I did not ask for a move, and had Burnley been willing to leave the matter for a time I might have been with them for the next season.

Soon I read that Sunderland were again interested. The rumour proved true, and on June 27, 1953, I joined the Roker Park club, at a reported £30,000 figure.

I was the third player bought by them within a few weeks, Ray Daniel and Jimmy Cowan being the others.

Tremendous publicity was given to this team-building, but the big-money tag did not worry me personally. True, I found it hard to settle, but that was just something which was cured by time.

You probably remember the disastrous season. We pulled clear of relegation only at the last minute. The reason was not *too many* stars, but that our styles would not blend immediately.

Suggestions of jealousy among us were nonsense. Almost every player in the first team had been bought—which provided a common bond—and our spirit was good.

If anything, we tried too hard. The fans naturally got annoyed at seeing so little after expecting so much.

The move to Sunderland meant a reunion with Len Shackleton, who had been a team-mate at Bradford.

There is no doubt about Shack's genius, but if he could play a little more straightforwardly I think he would have a place as the greatest inside forward in the game.

A flashback to Burnley to tell you of my happiest day—April 25, 1952.

That day was a Friday. It started miserably with a fire which brought out the local brigade, and put the house into an awful mess.

Everyone was in a flap when there was a knock at the door. I was surprised to see manager Frank Hill.

He told me Les Shannon had been selected for an England "B" touring party.

Then he added: "And you are in the main England party."

I was dumbfounded at those magical words . . . which led to my first cap, against Italy.

SUNDERLAND :

Standing—Daniel, Purdon, Anderson, Fraser, Hedley, McDonald.
Sitting—Bingham, Fleming, Aitken, Chisholm, Shackleton.

CHARLIE FLEMING, of
Sunderland and Scotland, says

They call me 'Cannonball'

AND I TRY TO
LIVE UP TO IT

I'VE hit plenty of goals in my time, and I'm hoping the future will bring me a lot more in English Soccer. My tally in Scotland when I left East Fife last January was 166 in just over 200 games.

From the moment I started playing I've made it my business to keep cracking at goal. I believe that the more you keep the goalkeepers on the hop, the more goals you will get.

Of course, a lot of shots go wide. Then you hear the crowd groan and jeer. But if one shot in five scores, it is a very, very good average.

I built up my shooting power—in Scotland I'm called "Cannonball"—by concentrated practice.

If any of Sunderland's goalkeepers want some overtime, I'm always willing to oblige. It gives me, as much as them, the chance to improve.

Naturally, some goals I have scored have brought more pleasure than others. There was one in particular, in a Scottish League Cup semi-final.

Famous Rangers were our opponents, a club East Fife had never beaten. At the end of normal time we shared two goals, and were a bit on edge, fearing they would push us out of a place in the final.

During extra time I got a pass on the 18-yard line, controlled the ball and smacked it as hard as I could. It was a wonderful moment to see the goalkeeper sprawling and the ball nestling in the bottom of the net.

Soon after that I got an unexpected honour. Although I'd never won an international cap, I was chosen for The Rest of the U.K. against Wales in a jubilee match.

We went down 3—2, but I got some satisfaction in putting a hot drive past Bill Shortt, the opposing keeper.

That match gave me the chance to partner Hibs' winger, Gordon Smith, for the first time. Originally, Tom Finney was selected, but he had to cry off. I had a lot of pleasure in linking with my fellow Scot.

Opportunism can change the course of a game in a flash. The best illustration I know of this was in the 1954 League Cup Final when East Fife met Partick Thistle.

Two up at half-time, we felt the match was ours. But Partick struck back and were level with four minutes left.

They looked like snatching a win. Then our right-half, Frank Christie, got the ball, steadied himself, and let rip a snorter from 25 yards. It was a winner from the moment he hit it.

My first international goals came in my debut for Scotland, against Ireland, at Windsor Park, Belfast, in 1954. Ireland did all the pressing, yet we won 3—1 because we were able to snap up scoring chances.

Now that I am in England I'm sorry I did not make an effort to get here earlier in my career. Pay is certainly better and conditions and facilities are a great improvement on Scotland. After East Fife, I find Roker Park most palatial.

All the time I was in Scottish Soccer I thought it would be pleasant to cross the border, but I never felt like chasing a transfer.

But the one occasion when I was really unsettled was at the start of the 1953-4 season, when I refused to re-sign. I wanted a small step-up in wages.

East Fife offered me £12 in the playing season, £10 in the summer. I asked for £12 all the year.

I did not get it, and eventually, deciding it was no use bucking all alone, put my name on the payroll.

Delighted though I was to join Sunderland, the move was not of my asking. Manager Gerry Dawson came to see me one Monday evening and asked if I fancied joining the Roker Park club.

Immediately I agreed—but the deal fell through. The following week it was "on" again, and I moved to the famous North East club in exchange for Tommy Wright and a fee.

My colleagues are a grand bunch. One of the first to greet me was the skipper, big George Aitken, who had been a team-mate of mine a few years earlier.

I also heard the Scottish accent from goalkeeper Bill Fraser and full-back Joe McDonald. Yet the player I palled up with was an Irishman—Billy Bingham.

Naturally, I wanted to get cracking with the League side as quickly as possible, but I didn't play a game for four weeks.

The club just could not find a place for me. So I travelled round as twelfth man.

My first game was at centre-forward—a position I had not occupied much before. We drew a goalless match at Blackpool and I got the chance to renew another old acquaintance with former team-mate Allan Brown.

A pleasant surprise about English Soccer is that I have found it little different from that at home. Certainly the players move the ball quicker. But the styles are the same.

There is one other difference. Scotland has no Len Shackleton. In fact, Len is one on his own.

I had thought him a great player when he opposed me. As a colleague, I can now really appreciate his superb ball control and ability to make openings.

" That's my boy-friend who has just scored ! "

He dialled M for McDonald

—and that happy phone call was the start of a new career for me

Says **JOE McDONALD**

Sunderland

THE phone rang and a voice said: "Don't take a heavy meal at lunchtime, you may be playing this afternoon."

It was Bert Johnston, Sunderland trainer, who spoke and that brief conversation was the start of a new career for me.

I did play on that Saturday afternoon, in April, 1954, against Sheffield United, as deputy for Jack Hedley, who was taken ill. It was my debut for Sunderland and a match for which I had waited a long time.

To join an English club had been my ambition from the day I signed as a part-timer for Bellshill Athletic.

True, we had great clubs in Scotland, but I felt that more opportunities lay across the border. Having made the grade in England, I'm even more firm in that opinion.

So, when Sunderland laid a contract before me as I sat in the Falkirk office with my manager Bob Shankley, I did not need any coaxing to sign.

For quite a time at Falkirk there had been rumours that English scouts were on my trail. I lived in hope, from day to day, that a transfer would come along.

★

After a game for Scotland "B" against the British Army, at Goodison Park, Liverpool, I felt really despondent.

It had been my chance to attract attention for there were dozens of managers and scouts in the stand. But I did not shine.

"You've thrown away a glorious chance," I thought on the train journey home.

Sunderland must have been satisfied, however, for soon afterwards I was on their payroll—just a day before goalkeeper Bill Fraser, who played against me in the Goodison Park match, moved to Roker Park.

It was a worrying time for Sunderland when we joined them on the eve of the transfer deadline. They had spent a huge sum on players but still faced relegation for the first time in their history. I was delighted to play a small part in helping them to safety.

As a youngster I played in goal. With Falkirk, right-back was usually my position, but at Sunderland I have mainly been on the other flank.

That switch has brought me against some great players of whom Stan Matthews, Tom Finney and Peter Harris are the outstanding trio of right-wingers.

The best summing up I can give of Matthews is that if he stops with the ball, and you are with him, he is always one move in advance. There can be few players to match his speed over 15 yards.

Finney, because of the unorthodox way he works the ball with his left foot, has a body swerve which makes you think he is going inside. Whichever way he goes he is very dangerous because, if you force him inside he is capable of finishing with a scoring shot.

Fastest is Portsmouth's Peter Harris.

" Clever, isn't it? People don't know whether I'm coming or going. "

It is his dynamic burst of speed which takes him through the most compact defences in a flash.

The Scottish right-winger nearest to these three is Gordon Smith, of Hibs. Like Finney and Harris he is capable of pulling out match-winning goals. I found him quite a handful.

Army football has helped me a lot. While stationed at Gibraltar I had plenty of opportunity to turn out in good-class games with Jack Lindsay, Morton outside-right, and Jack Neilson, St. Mirren wing-half.

I was usually picked in one of the inside-forward positions. I thoroughly enjoyed it and profited by the experience.

It gave me a much clearer idea of tactical moves in the position and, when I returned to full-back, I was often able to anticipate what a rival forward would do.

★

More valuable experience came my way when I was chosen for an international trial, under floodlight, against Kilmarnock.

This was one of a series of games played before the important match with Hungary, and although Harry Haddock (Clyde) finally got into the side I had some consolation by being chosen as reserve.

All the Sunderland players have played their part in helping me settle at the club. Despite the big money tags many of them bear, they all realise it is only good play which will keep them in the team.

I found magnificent spirit in the dressing-room from the first day I was issued with a blue and white track suit.

Having direct playing link with Bill Fraser and George Aitken—two fellow countrymen—has undoubtedly helped my play. Fraser would give any full-back confidence—he is so safe.

I also know that if I should be beaten, Big George, whose words of encouragement are a tonic in a tight corner, will probably be around to help out.

JACK HEDLEY
Sunderland

TALKING IT OVER ... *by JOHN THOMPSON*

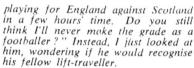

Clown
or
Genius ?

I F I was an average footballer I would not be overjoyed if I was asked to partner Leonard Francis Shackleton—I would not know what to expect from this self-styled clown prince of Soccer.

Sometimes he shocks his own supporters with performances that would not earn him a place in a Third Division team. Often he is such a genius that he would clearly be too brilliant for pedestrian members of the England side.

He is a shocking fellow altogether, brimming over with impudence, uncanny skill, and assorted humours. He is a character in a game which generally lacks characters, and he provokes feelings which are as strong as those he feels himself. **He is Len Shackleton of Sunderland and England, and he is unique.**

His character is a strange mixture, and his experiences have been mixed, too, blending the man that he now is for good or ill.

As a boy, he had high dreams.

There we were, sitting in Sunday school, when our teacher asked each member of the class in turn, " What would you like to be when you grow up ? " It came to my turn, and I told him outright, " I'm going to be a footballer." He was not impressed.

Shackleton tells of that moment in his book* which has recently been published. As you might expect, it is the sauciest and most provocative book ever to be written by a star footballer. It will cause more controversy than all the rest put together.

It has its human side, too. It is revealing, as few sporting autobiographies are, in the thoughts that make him tick. There are the memories here which have formed Shackleton's outlook and his opinion, his wit and his agility of mind and body.

There was the thrill of signing for mighty Arsenal and the day when he learned that his dreams were in vain.

Then followed an interview I shall never forget. With each pronouncement the facts became clearer. I was washed up, was not good enough for Arsenal—or any other club for that matter ; I would have to return to Bradford and become, perhaps, a miner, an engineer, perhaps a commercial traveller—but never a footballer.

Years later, as he prepared for an international match in Glasgow, Shackleton met Arsenal manager George Allison again.

On entering the lift to go to my room, I noticed the only other occupant was Allison. It was a big temptation to point out to him, " I shall be

★

LEN SHACKLETON, Clown Prince of Soccer. His Autobiography. Edited by David R. Jack. Published by Nicholas Kaye, London, at 10s. 6d.

playing for England against Scotland in a few hours' time. Do you still think I'll never make the grade as a footballer ? " Instead, I just looked at him, wondering if he would recognise his fellow lift-traveller.

A trifle small, you think ? And then that impish humour, directed often at himself, restores our sympathy a little with the wayward author, for he adds :

England were beaten 1—0, and I had a poor match, endorsing, perhaps, the Arsenal manager's original opinion about my football ability.

Selected for an international match, Shackleton pondered whether to play . . .

I decided to play, and it still amuses me to imagine what the feelings of the Football Association would have been had they known that I represented England for the sake of publicity as much as for the honour of wearing the international shirt !

What kind of taste does that leave in the mouth ? Would the boy who had such dreams of Soccer fame have stomached such sentiments ? They are human enough, certainly, formed by his life and by his disappointments.

Perhaps all of us would feel the same way. I don't know. But if we felt that way, would we *write* about it for the dreaming youngsters of today to digest ? I wonder.

Shackleton attacks the opinion of England captain Billy Wright, who is so dedicated to the game itself that he has given unforgettable service to his club and country.

I have read a book written by Billy Wright, England's Soccer skipper. Billy states in that book, " If there was nothing else but the inducement of an international cap, I would be just as eager to play for England." I consider his sentiments ludicrous, because when a man is playing football for a living, he must be paid in sterling—unless he

intends to exist on the trophies the game provides.

But how many footballers, with all their hard-bitten talk, would agree with Wright—and how many with Shackleton ?

Watch any lad who has just been told that his country has honoured him, and I doubt if you will find him reckoning up the cash he will receive. It is not Wright's view that is ludicrous.

But players in " show " games should be paid better than they are, and in this I am in complete agreement with Shackleton.

And here is his sardonic view of the transfer system :

I may be wrong, but it seems rather absurd to have people bartering in human flesh, without so much as permitting the object of their bids to be present at the sale. Even harem-bound girls were permitted to sum up their prospective employers while the bidding was taking place.

He buzzes around England selectors like an angry wasp, stinging sometimes with bitter irony. And sometimes he hits out with a sledgehammer.

Once a selector was asked why Shackleton was consistently left out of the team.

The answer was smart enough ; in fact, I suppose I should have been flattered : " Because we play at Wembley Stadium, not the London Palladium ! "

But perhaps the most scathing comment of all in the book is a blank page. It is headed :

Chapter 9. The Average Director's Knowledge of Football.

And underneath the white space is the note :

This chapter has deliberately been left blank in accordance with the author's wishes.

It was typical of Shackleton that he should write a shocking book and ask Bill Murray to write an introduction to it soon after the Sunderland manager had given him a dressing-down.

SUNDERLAND UNDER THE SPOTLIGHT !

Lofthouse the Bolton centre-forward flashes this effort wide off Willie Fraser the visiting keeper.

Fraser dives to thwarts this Tottenham attack.

Don Revie, Sunderland's international link man.

Len Shackleton in close up action.

Charles Buchan's FOOTBALL MONTHLY

APRIL 1955

1'6

Overseas Price 2/-
Forces Overseas 1/6

Exclusive articles by :—
VIC METCALFE
ALLENBY CHILTON
REG MATTHEWS
CHARLIE TULLY
JIMMY BAXTER
BOBBY MITCHELL
BILLY ELLIOTT
EDDIE STUART
JIMMY JACKSON
HARRY HADDOCK
JACK GRAINGER

LEN SHACKLETON
Sunderland
and England

Money Isn't

Everything

What is it like to be a £10 player in a team which cost £150,000? Are the expensive types any better, and different from the others? The answer is "No." But read on . . .

by *STAN ANDERSON* (Sunderland)

DOES a player change when he gets a big transfer rating? I don't think so. For a long time I was the only locally produced product in a Sunderland side supposed to have cost about £150,000. I found the stars around me just the same as any players who have not cost a penny over the £10 signing-on fee.

I must admit that when I was promoted to that glittering array of talent, I was nervous. Soon, however, I got to know my colleagues, and they did all they could to help me.

Many laughed and joked about the money spent on them. They did not welcome all the cash talk, I can assure you, and they needed a bit of banter to keep up their spirits when we struck a particularly bad patch.

Sunderland now have a junior team, and seem to possess some young players of talent. But when I broke through the barrier to the senior side, in October, 1952, it was a rare thing for a home-grown product to win his way to the top.

As a schoolboy international I always admired Ken Willingham. I regarded him as the ideal to follow.

I was 18 when I got that wonderful jump into the League team. As a part-timer I trained at night, and when I checked in one Thursday evening and found myself promoted, I just wanted to run all the way home with the news.

It happened because Willie Watson was reserve for England and George Aitken was unfit . . . so I was put in, against Portsmouth. My opponent was Len Phillips, a great inside-forward—but not the best I have faced. Without doubt, Aston Villa's Johnny Dixon is the player who gives the most trouble. Strong, fast

and quick to spot an opening, he is one of the most under-rated players in the game.

In my early games with Sunderland's first team I owed a lot to Arthur Wright—now in charge of Sunderland's juniors—who often pulled me to one side and passed on tips.

Arthur didn't talk a lot, but he was always tremendously keen and willing to help others. And to a youngster fighting his way along, a few words from an established player are of immense benefit.

In some games I played behind Len Shackleton. I found no difficulty in linking with him, despite his very unorthodox style. When Len wanted the ball he called for it. But he shouted only when there was an opening.

In season 1953-4 I won a permanent place in the team despite the arrival of more "name" players—like Jimmy Cowan, Billy Elliott, Ray Daniel and Ken Chisholm.

That was the season when Sunderland almost lost thir proud record of having never played in any League but the First Division.

Were we top-heavy with stars? Was there dressing-room jealousy? The answer is a definite "no."

Time for several quick ones—for the game is over. And here sinking welcome lemonades are Bingham, Stelling and Wright—while Shackleton (left) looks on.

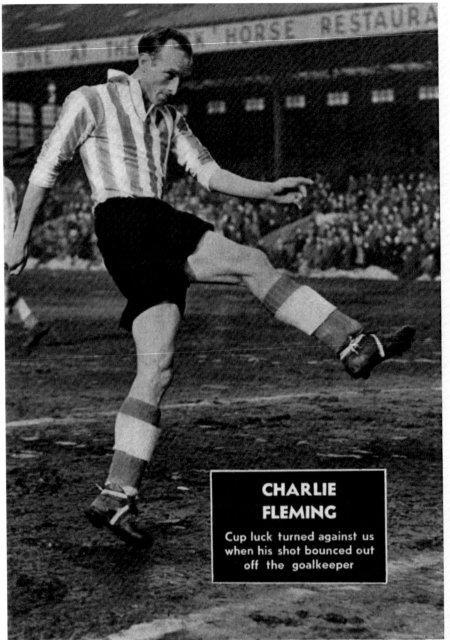

CHARLIE FLEMING

Cup luck turned against us when his shot bounced out off the goalkeeper

A few months later we were battling towards Wembley. A highlight Cup tussle was against Preston when we drew 3-3 in what I think was the outstanding inter-club game I have played.

Shack got a goal that day, a gloriously placed chip shot, over the goalkeeper's head.

★

Drawn against Manchester City in the semi-final, we felt certain the Cup would be ours. Luck turned its back at Villa Park, after only ten minutes, when Charlie Fleming shot, Bert Trautmann dived the wrong way—and the ball bounced clear after hitting him.

Had it gone in I'm sure we would not have lost by a single goal.

★

My short League career has certainly been packed with excitement. Jostling with the stars, tussling for the championship and F.A. Cup, I've also played for England " B " team and the under 23's, and been reserve for the full international side.

What more could a young player want? Well I'd like to follow Ken Willingham's steps all the way—and win a cap.

BILLY ELLIOTT . . . one of the many star players to arrive at Sunderland

Everyone fought hard, it was all for one and one for all. Although we played well at times, luck seemed right against us. That we were a useful side was proved in the following season when we were in the thick of the fight for League and Cup honours.

It was a worrying time, however, for relegation became a possibility. Hard-earned points at first seemed likely to take us clear, but we slumped and, with only three matches left, were in trouble.

Playing Sheffield United, at Roker Park, we were 2-1 down when a penalty was awarded us ten minutes from time. I was told to take it and my legs turned into jelly.

I managed to conquer my nerves, however, and put the ball safely past the goalkeeper, into the corner of the net.

That kick brought us a precious point, but I often wonder what would have happened had I missed. Thank goodness I no longer take penalty kicks. The spotkicker has a thankless task.

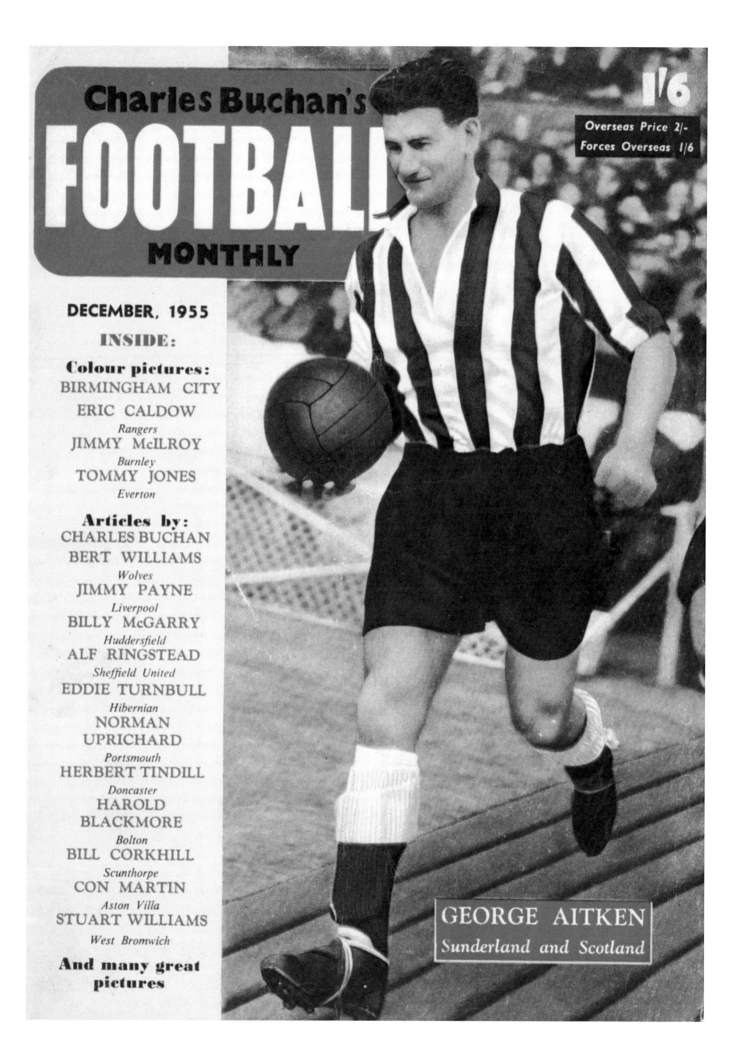

Charles Buchan's FOOTBALL MONTHLY

1/6

Overseas Price 2/-
Forces Overseas 1/6

DECEMBER, 1955

INSIDE:

Colour pictures:
BIRMINGHAM CITY
ERIC CALDOW
Rangers
JIMMY McILROY
Burnley
TOMMY JONES
Everton

Articles by:
CHARLES BUCHAN
BERT WILLIAMS
Wolves
JIMMY PAYNE
Liverpool
BILLY McGARRY
Huddersfield
ALF RINGSTEAD
Sheffield United
EDDIE TURNBULL
Hibernian
NORMAN UPRICHARD
Portsmouth
HERBERT TINDILL
Doncaster
HAROLD BLACKMORE
Bolton
BILL CORKHILL
Scunthorpe
CON MARTIN
Aston Villa
STUART WILLIAMS
West Bromwich

And many great pictures

GEORGE AITKEN
Sunderland and Scotland

by JACK HEDLEY
Sunderland

BOGOTA! the full story of my trip

EVERTON to Sunderland is not a particularly exciting journey—if you take the most direct route. But vary things a little by travelling via Bogota, as I did, and you will have something to be long remembered.

For some other players the South American jaunt proved a Bogota blunder. For me it ended happily—and rather surprisingly. Here, for the first time, are the full background details.

★　　★　　★

Before Everton went on a close season tour in 1950, to Sweden, my club-mate Billy Higgins told me of an offer he had received from the Millionairos Club.

I was not specially interested, and so got a shock on returning to England to find that Billy had completed a dollar deal and gone to South America.

Soon a cable arrived from him. He said everything seemed all right. I did not, however, accept his invitation to join him --and soon received a more urgent cable, telling me to get out there by a certain date.

I made up my mind to have a look at Bogota, but after making quick arrangements I found that my inoculations were not in order.

Next step was a message to contact Jock Dodds, who was acting as agent.

Let me make one point quite clear about the Scottish international centre-forward—he believed he was paving the way to great opportunity.

One night he drove Roy Paul and me through darkness to Glasgow, and we started on our way to the unknown. Two days later we touched down in Bogota.

Billy met us, and he did not paint a picture of paradise.

"It's not bad, but more English players are needed," he said. "On your own you will be frozen out of the game.

"**Be careful what you sign,**" he added. "**I thought I was signing for photographs, but now I'm tied to this club and cannot move.**"

So far . . . not so good. But the position became worse.

★

Soon we met Neil Franklin and George Mountford, who were with the Santa Fe club. They asked what terms we were getting.

"That's hardly enough to live on," they gasped, when we mentioned the figure. "You'll have to ask for a lot more."

Roy and I got hold of an interpreter and some club officials and decided on a show down. We got no satisfaction, and immediately decided on a quick return home.

Roy had hardly any spare kit, and I only possessed a spare shirt and shaving kit.

Bogota is a nice place, nine thousand feet up. But the air made breathing

(Continued on page 12)

JACK HEDLEY . . . who reached Sunderland from Everton via Bogota.

One of Hedley's greatest disappointments was Sunderland's defeat by Manchester City in the 1955 Cup semi-final. And here is the goal which upset him.

(Continued from page 11)

very difficult until you became well acclimatised.

Playing football was terribly strenuous because of the air. And another snag was that the fans expected the English players to rival performing seals and be a mixture of the Stan Matthews-Len Shackleton ball genius.

But how were we to get back home? Fortunately, Millionairos paid the fare, and we got some dollars from the Santa Fe president. We were thus able to pay for bare necessities on the trip via Jamaica, Miami, New York and Paris.

Back in Liverpool, I wondered what Everton would think about my journey.

Immediately on arrival I visited Goodison Park. There, Mr. Cliff Britton said the board would have to make a decision and that he would pass it on to me.

The next move came from Sunderland. Manager Bill Murray came to my home and asked if I would like to join the Roker Park club.

"I don't know whether I'm for transfer," I replied. "Oh, we've permission to approach you," he said.

It was a shock, and before I made a decision I went to Everton to clear up a few points. Eventually, I signed for Sunderland; it meant playing nearer to my north-east home.

Now, Everton had been a defensively-minded team . . . Sunderland thought on attacking lines. So I got off to a bad start.

My debut was at Liverpool—just a mile away from my former club. I came up against Billy Liddell in top form, and though I had previously held my own in our tussles, he gave me an awful tousing this time.

He scored two goals, made another, and so unsettled me that two games later I was dropped.

Some months passed before I returned, against Derby County in a fantastic game which they won 6—5. My next match was against Liverpool, and I determined that Liddell would not " come his capers " again.

★

Fortunately, the ball ran more kindly for me, and the confidence this brought was a big help in restoring my form.

The many big-money players Sunderland signed a few seasons ago brought a lot of publicity, which wasn't, however, of any help to the team.

Although, on the surface, the lads never seemed to bother about their transfer prices, I am sure they were a mental worry, and upset their approach to the game.

I consider that to be the reason for the long time it took the players to blend together.

Two matches which we lost by single goals—against Manchester City and Moscow Dynamo—were among the biggest disappointments of my career.

We were confident of beating City in the 1955 Cup semi-final, and their late winner was a blow.

So, too, was our unimpressive display against the Russians. Had we struck anything like real form we would have won soundly, for they were only a very average side.

Build A Fine Library

Why not build up a grand Soccer library with a " set " of Football Monthlies ? Many of our readers treasure their collections and tell us that these magazines will give pleasure to themselves and their sons for many years to come.

A limited supply of back numbers is now available. If some of yours are missing all you need do to add to your collection is to send 1s. 6d. for each copy required to : Charles Buchan, 408, Strand, W.C.2. They will then be sent to you post free.

Issues available are : Willie Moir (July, 1954), George Farm (October), Jack Mansell (November), World Cup player faints (December), Sam Bartram (January, 1955), Ray Wood (February), Dave Ewing (March), Jimmy Meadows (May), Bert Williams (June), Goalmouth Scene (July), Billy Wright (August), George Thompson (September), Stanley Matthews (October), Ken Taylor (November), George Aitken (December), Doug Holden (January, 1956), Eddie Lowe and John Atyeo (February), Ron Baynham (March).

Some overseas readers may have difficulty in obtaining " Football Monthly " regularly, and we suggest that in their own interest, they become annual subscribers. An international money order for £1 6s. 0d. sterling may be purchased in the currency of your country at most banks and post offices and this can be forwarded to us.

Subscriptions (per annum): Inland £1 1s. 6d., overseas £1 6s. 0d., special overseas Forces rate £1 1s. 6d., dollar rate from U.S.A. and Canada 3.75 dollars. Orders and remittances to : Hulton Press Ltd., Subscription Branch, Long Lane, Aintree, Liverpool, 9.

It is possible to have any twelve copies bound in luxurious book form. After you have completed sets of twelve send them for binding, enclosing 12s. to cover costs and postage to : Messrs. T. W. Coleman, 3 Wine Office Court, Fleet Street, London, E.C.4.

Riot ? No, Cup-tie fever !

★ Delirious with the fever of triumph following their team's 2—0 Cup win over Newcastle, the holders, Sunderland fans swarm over the pitch to mob their heroes. Below, Simpson, Newcastle goalkeeper, punches away a Sunderland corner. Note the people perched on the roof-top. ★

by BILL HOLDEN
Sunderland

WHEN a player asks for a transfer, especially if he has lost his place in the first team, he is usually criticised. Rarely does anyone back him up.

Yet I think that in the majority of cases he dislikes seeking a transfer. There is nothing he really desires less than uprooting himself from among friends to make a fresh start in another town.

Take my case which I do not think is an isolated example. Until the 1955-56 season I was regular leader of Burnley.

In August, 1955, I started off against Tottenham hoping for a good scoring season. A couple of days later I played against Blackpool . . . and little did it occur to me that I would never again be in the Burnley first team.

But I was dropped and could not regain my place. After a time I asked for a move. It was not annoyance at being replaced by Peter McKay ; he was doing a good job.

The real reason was that I could not strike form. I had no zest or zip for the Saturday afternoon match and felt a change was needed to bring back the form which had deserted me.

During the previous close season I had decided to have a complete rest from all ball games. Normally I play golf or tennis to try and keep fit.

This time I had a lazy, leisurely break hoping to report back to Turf Moor full of enthusiasm and keen to get out with a football.

I needed a tonic – and the move to Sunderland gave it me!

My plan must have misfired. The rest appeared to do more harm than good and I just could not get going.

Do you think I was happy at this state of affairs ? Wouldn't you be upset if you found it hard to do your job and everything seemingly going wrong ? Remember football is my living ; it is not just a game. Loss of form is a terrible mental trouble and when I was dropped I struggled in the reserves and worried constantly.

I really began to believe that different surroundings might provide the tonic to shake up my old enthusiasm.

And how I needed a tonic ! I reached such a state that even my hobbies meant nothing. All the time my mind was on football. The more I tried to put myself right, the more I seemed to be in a maze.

Eventually Burnley agreed to my request. There was one club I would have liked to join—Blackpool. Apart from the thought of the bracing air there, I considered it would be marvellous to lead an attack containing so many great players.

"How many more nights are you going to waste trying to get some Cup tickets?"

That dream did not come true, and a move anywhere seemed unlikely until Boxing Day came along.

I had watched Burnley play Preston in the afternoon and was at home when a message came from Manager Alan Brown asking me to report at the ground.

It was such an odd time I felt something unusual must be happening. Arriving at Turf Moor I was asked if I would consider going half way to Sunderland to meet officials of that club.

I agreed to do so and we got together some hours later in a Ripon hotel. It was hard to make a decision. I had the opportunity of the change I wanted . . . but Sunderland was a long way from home.

After talking it over with my fiancée—we are now married—we decided to take a chance.

On to Seaburn I went to stay the night, or what little remained of it, in another hotel prior to playing against Newcastle United a few hours later.

Sunderland hoped this match might bring them revenge for the heavy defeat on the previous day.

No announcement was made about my transfer, although the Newcastle team soon realised I was playing ; it was quite a shock to the crowd, too.

I managed to give them another shock after six minutes by scoring. Unfortunately we did not get the run of the ball and instead of earning at least a point, we lost 3—1.

Injuries can be really worrying. In 1952 I played against Derby County and got a crack on the side of my left leg. I could not train all week but the following Friday I had a try-out and felt I would be all right.

During the first few minutes I got another knock. I tried to flick the ball and my leg simply gave way.

Off to hospital I went—having goalkeeper Joe McNulty, another casualty, with me, for an X-ray which showed a break.

Fortunately the injury happened in March and by getting manipulative treatment I was fit for the start of the next season.

When it was completely mended the injured leg seemed stronger than the other and proof of its 100 per cent recovery came in selection, a year later, for the England " B " team against Scotland.

What "Monty" didn't know

when he shook hands with me was that I was absent without leave from the Army

by

WILLIE FRASER

Sunderland
and Scotland

DOWN the lines of Portsmouth and Sunderland players, at Fratton Park, walked Field Marshal Viscount Montgomery. He had a handshake for each player, including me—although I was Absent without Leave from my unit.

Of course, "Monty" did not know that. Nor did anyone else at the ground. I'd taken the gamble and gone hookey, that day in September, 1954, because I did not mean to miss this important match.

I was just about to be demobbed and, as football is such an up and down business, I wanted to be quite sure of keeping my place.

Deputies have a habit of stepping in and doing well.

When I returned to camp I was "docked" a day's pay, and lost a stripe.

But I was well able to stand the cash loss because that match helped me impress the international selectors. A month later I got my first cap, against Wales, and with it £50 match fee.

First news I had of the honour came from a newspaper seller's poster.

On the night before the team was chosen I played my farewell game for the Army against Rangers. Before the team was announced (next day) I had left Glasgow.

Back near Sunderland, some hours later, I saw the poster and couldn't get out of the car quick enough to buy a newspaper and read the team.

Incidentally I set a record by being the first Australian-born player to win a Scottish cap.

My Sunderland colleagues warned me to watch out for bustling centre-forward Trevor Ford, who had previously been at Roker Park.

I was certainly surprised by the Welsh leader—he was so subdued. We won 1—0, with a magnificent flying header from centre-forward Paddy Buckley.

The hardest game I have ever had was when I captained the Army team on a German tour. We were due to play a Select XI, according to the fixture list.

Select! I'll say it was! Our opponents turned out to be the complete World Cup championship team. I had heard Germany were lucky to win the trophy, but there was no doubting their outstanding ability when we played them.

The attack of Rahn, Morlock, the two Walters, and Schaeffer packed such powerful shooting that eventually I hurt my wrist and had to play on the left wing.

We were a pretty useful side but never got into this match with a chance, and lost 8—0.

Incidentally, our left-back was a player I think certain to win Welsh fame and honours—Mel Hopkins, of Spurs.

Others in our side were Frank Blunstone (Chelsea), Ron Clayton (Blackburn), Phil Gunter (Portsmouth), and Swansea's strong Melvyn Charles.

Two people who have helped me a lot during my career—former Airdrie manager, Willie Fotheringham, and Sunderland inside - forward, Len Shackleton.

Fotheringham, a top-flight keeper himself, spent a lot of time showing me tactical moves, when I was at his club.

Len's help has been more theoretical, but none the less valuable.

A goalkeeper—unlike full-backs, half-backs or forwards—has no partner to discuss his play with. But Shack has a brilliant knowledge of goalkeeping—probably because of his close friendship with former Newcastle keeper Jack Fairbrother.

So, returning from matches, and in training sessions, I often seek his advice.

My transfer to Sunderland was a real hustle. I was stationed at Stirling in March, 1954, when I got a 'phone call asking me if I would like to go to Roker Park.

The following day came another message, telling me to report at the Airdrie ground as quickly as possible.

It was the last day for transfers to be valid that season so, when I got out of camp, I tore to the club and signed immediately.

When the business was completed I was off again, back to Stirling, to catch the night train to Bristol where I was playing the next day, for the Army.

I was a little sorry to leave the happy band at Airdrie, but delightedly made my English debut against Tottenham Hotspur, a few days later.

We beat Spurs 1—0 and my day was completed by Ray Daniel as he congratulated me in the dressing room.

"Bebe," as we call the famous centre-half, said: "Anyone who can play behind me is darned good."

It was a laugh at himself—but a nice tribute to me.

Billy Bingham, my close pal at the club, scored a goal against me, in my second international, against Ireland. It was a real upset.

A harmless ball came to me and seeing Willie McNaught apparently alone, I threw the ball to him.

As it left my hand I would have given anything to pull it back for, round Willie's back popped a fair head. It was Irishman Billy, who promptly nipped past the defender, controlled the ball and put in a smashing drive.

It was a good shot but not the hardest I have met. Of the players I have faced, Jackie Milburn has the fiercest shooting power.

On two occasions when he beat me I barely saw the ball. The first time was in an Army match with the F.A. The other was in a "derby" game against Newcastle.

" It's our wedding anniversary and I promised to spend the whole day with her ! "

SAMUEL KEMP

COLIN GRAINGER

LEN SHACKLETON

SUNDERLAND STARS

JOE McDONALD

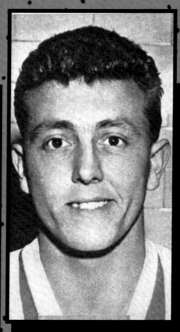

HARRY CLARK

WILLIE MORRISON

ALBUM OF ACTION

Sailing high as a bird (or so it seems) above Roker Park's crowded terraces and flag standard is Preston winger Mayers as he makes a magnificent leap above Hedley, of Sunderland.

COLIN GRAINGER
**Sunderland
and England**

POOR OLD JOE! HIM BUT HE WITH A GRIN

by RAY DANIEL
Sunderland and Wales

When I look back I recall many moments when I felt regret and pleasure together. Perhaps my most upsetting time was when I scored a goal which knocked our old colleague's team out of the Cup. I shall never forget what he said.

I WAS just a youngster of seventeen when I left the informal atmosphere of cosy Third Division club Swansea Town for the elaborate Highbury set-up.

It was a big step to take, but when you are setting out on a professional Soccer career you don't hesitate if you have made up your mind where you want to be.

At Highbury I first made contact with those Arsenal giants of the time, Leslie and Denis Compton, Walley Barnes, Joe Mercer, Laurie Scott, Jimmy Logie, George Swindin and Doug Lishman.

It was a great team at Highbury in every sense of the word, and a youngster gets a big welcome there and has the use of the vast facilities. But it did not take me long to realise that I would have to work very hard to reach the astonishing standard set by the men who were carrying on from where the pre-war Arsenal side had left off.

After I had been there a year or two I knew that it would take patience to go on filling the role of understudy to Leslie Compton, a truly great player in the tradition of Arsenal centre-halves.

I had been picked for a number of First Division games as reserve-on-call before one of the odd twists with which Soccer abounds brought me a "cap" for my country while I was still only reserve for my club.

Leslie Compton received his first England cap in the same game.

To cap it all, the match took place at Roker Park, where, three years later, I was to step out with Sunderland on the next stage of my career.

After the England v. Wales match, events moved quickly for me. By the end of the season I was first choice for club and country.

Then a League championship medal and a losing Cup Final appearance at Wembley—still a great thrill despite that unlucky 1-0 defeat by Newcastle United—followed in quick succession.

At the end of the 1952-53 season came the chance of a move to Sunderland . . . another important step in my career.

I felt a twinge of regret at leaving the great-hearted Highbury "old guard," who had been such wonderful colleagues and companions.

They had given me the helping hand so freely while

I HAD BEATEN STOOD THERE ON HIS FACE

I was climbing to the top; now they wished me luck with another club and were just as anxious that I should come out on top in the move which I elected to make.

I needed those best wishes, too, for right from the start of the 1953-54 season—I had signed for Sunderland during the close season with Billy Elliott, from Burnley, and Jimmy Cowan, from Morton—things simply wouldn't go right.

The jinx was there with a vengeance from the first kick. We had started with a sensational game against Charlton, at The Valley. We were 3-1 down after 21 minutes, drew level at 3-3 but lost 5-3.

In the following games we tried all we knew to settle down into the unbeatable combination which, on the score of experience and ability, we should have been.

At the back of my mind all the time was the thought that there had been quite a lot of criticism of my decision to leave Arsenal. People told me that I would regret it.

But I still thought I had done the right thing. I wanted to prove it, too, but before I had had the chance to do so, and while my new club were still the target of heavy criticism on all sides for the moderate start they had made to the season, our League game with Arsenal came up for decision.

You can imagine how I felt about lining up against my old colleagues before I had really got my teeth into my new job.

My old club-mates would want to show me where I had gone wrong—and I was just as desperately keen to prove that I was right.

After just 25 minutes that sinking feeling was there again when Doug Lishman popped up to shoot Arsenal into the lead.

Before half-time, however, Trevor Ford and Billy Elliott made it 2-1. And then in the second half, a rush of five goals in 19 minutes by Len Shackleton, Ford (2), and Tommy Wright (2), made it a rousing 7-1 triumph for Sunderland.

A team triumph, yes, but no one was more in need of that boost in morale than Ray Daniel.

Yet Arsenal were once my club and the shattering blow which we dealt them that day sent them to the bottom-of-the-League position for the first time in many years.

In the following season we went to Swansea in the fifth round of the Cup and forced a 2-2 draw at the Vetch Field, where you first have to win your battles against the fervour of the Welsh crowd before you get down to winning the match.

With Ronnie Burgess to spur them on, Swansea were a great team that day and we were quite happy to force a replay, which we won 1-0.

It was good to finish on top, even at the second attempt. But again I had to spare a thought for my old club, who had put up a really magnificent fight.

A near miss ! Ray Daniel (centre of picture) looks back anxiously as his goalkeeper, Willie Fraser, hurls himself at the ball—which, fortunately for Sunderland, was the wrong side of the post.

The price of fame !   Brought to a standstill by young fans, Billy Elliott (you can see his middle-parting on the left) goes to work with his pen. Len Shackleton, however, seems to be smiling through the throng.

Perhaps the most touching flash-back of all came when we were paired with Sheffield United in the fifth round of the Cup.

On a snow-covered pitch at Bramall Lane we forced a 0-0 draw. On Monday the sixth round draw was made and out of the hat came a trip to our North-East neighbours, Newcastle United.

After the previous season's heart-breaking experience of being knocked out in the semi-final by Manchester City, we were keyed-up to make sure of a trip to Wembley this time.

But first there was the Sheffield United replay hurdle to clear. United had shown plenty of fight at Bramall Lane and they were just as difficult to pin down at Roker Park.

After a goal-less first half, the minutes were ticking away and we had still not found a way through. It was one of those games when you felt that one goal would be enough to win.

Two teams sparred anxiously, giving nothing away. Then it happened. Just seven minutes from the end, Len Shackleton—always ready to seize the advantage with a quick move after a stoppage—took a throw-in on the left.

★

He sent the ball back to McDonald, who promptly stroked it forward to George Aitken.

I was just leaving the centre circle when Aitken's square pass reached me. I had already made up my mind what I was going to do. The ball came to me just right and I hit a hard, rising shot from 40 yards.

Ted Burgin, United's goalkeeper, could not have expected it for he was just a fraction of a second late in moving as the ball flashed into the top right-hand corner of the net for the match-winning goal.

It is the thrill of a lifetime to score a goal like that. What a kick it gave me. But, when the final whistle sounded and we trooped off the field, I felt the first tug at my heart-strings.

For there, waiting on the touch-line with a broad grin and outstretched arms to congratulate me, was the manager of the beaten team—my old Arsenal friend and adviser, Joe Mercer.

" Sorry, Joe, anyone but you . . ." I began. But Joe said : " Forget it, Ray. That was a goal in a million . . . the best I've ever seen."

It is good to win, especially in the Cup. But generous Joe Mercer, in his first season as manager of Sheffield United, really touched me with his warm praise of a goal which struck him a heavy blow.

When I look back to that game I still have a touch of regret.

BILLY ELLIOTT . . . " was one of the 'new boys' with me at Sunderland."

JOHNNY BOLLANDS
Sunderland

Charles Buchan's
FOOTBALL
MONTHLY

BILLY BINGHAM
Sunderland and Ireland

A-C-T-I-O-N!
scenes that capture some of the thrills of an exciting season . . .

High in the sky leaps Swansea goal-keeper King, to take the ball from the head of Goodchild, of Sunderland. Charles is on the spot — in case.

Charles Buchan's
FOOTBALL
MONTHLY

1/6
Overseas Price 2/-
Forces Overseas 1/6

OCTOBER
1956

CHARLIE
FLEMING
Sunderland
and Scotland

Stan Anderson

Season 1956-57 began badly and got worse. A constantly changing line-up only added to the confusion. Willie Fraser was replaced in goal by Johnny Bollands, after conceding six in an opening day defeat to Luton Town. In November, with the team down in twenty first place, there was one final flourish of the cheque book, with the signing of Don Revie from Manchester City.

Relegation had long looked on the cards as a dispirited bunch of players lurched from crisis to crisis, but somehow they found the resolve to lift themselves out of the relegation zone with an unbeaten run of seven games as the campaign reached its conclusion, and given what was happening behind the scenes at the club, this was remarkable..

Towards the end of 1956, the Football League had received an anonymous letter alleging financial irregularities at the club. The letter was signed simply Smith, but contained such convincing details, that the League were forced to act, and they descended on Roker Park, demanding to examine 'the books'. At this time in English football, there were strict rules about wages, signing on fees and bonuses.

Following this investigation, on the 7th of March, 1957, a six man commission formed jointly by the Football League and the Football Association, interviewed the Sunderland chairman Ted Ditchburn, director W.S. Martin,

manager Bill Murray and secretary George Crow in Sheffield.

Three weeks later, the commission then summoned the entire Sunderland board, as well as Murray and Crow, to a further meeting at York. Also instructed to attend, was a solicitor, representing a firm of contractors regularly used by the club for ground maintenance.

On April 10th, with the team teetering on the brink of relegation, the commission published its findings.

They made sensational reading.

Basically the commission reported that the club had been making enormous illicit payments to players, to 'bribe' them to join, totalling £5,427 14s 2d over the previous years. They had been covering this up by secretly overpaying the contractors for work invoiced. The contractors then reimbursed the club in cash, and this cash had then been used to make the illegal payments to the players.

Ted Ditchburn and W.S. Martin were suspended permanently from any involvement in football. Two other directors were suspended sine die, and all the rest of the board were severely censored, whilst the club itself was handed the biggest ever fine imposed in British football £5,000.

This was not the end of the matter. On the 16th April, The F.A. named the guilty players. They were Ray Daniel, Billy Elliott, Willie Fraser and Johnny Hannigan, plus two others who

had by now left the club, Trevor Ford and Ken Chisholm.

All turned up a meeting at the F.A. except for Trevor Ford who was by now playing in Holland, and all the players, under advice from their solicitors, refused to answer any questions.

All five of them were suspended sine die, but three weeks later, after the players finally admitted taking the money, their suspensions were lifted.

Manager Bill Murray was fined £200, and felt that under the circumstances, he couldn't continue, so he subsequently handed in his resignation to the newly appointed chairman, Colonel John Turnbull. Murray had come clean during the investigation, and had, among his revelations, told the commission that he had handed Trevor Ford a brown parcel containing £250. The player continued to deny it, and in consequence, he was banned from English football for three years.

Surprisingly, Sunderland received a fair amount of sympathy from the wider football community, a case of: 'But for the grace of God.' The maximum wage structure and bonus system were largely considered to be out of date, and in reality, the system was probably being widely abused by many other clubs.

Despite all the turmoil, the players had managed to accumulate enough points to stay up, finishing three points clear in twentieth spot.

SUNDERLAND SOCCER BOMBSHELL FROM PAGE ONE

MANAGER MURRAY NAMES ONE PLAYER WHO HAD ILLEGAL PAYMENT, PROMISES FULL DETAILS

Cardington King's fine victory

Pegg on wing for Man. U.

The quest for a new manager began, and with it, the need to restore the club's tarnished reputation. Alan Brown was the choice. A respected figure within the game, he was considered to be enigmatic at best, and a most difficult character to work with at worst, but he was honest and hard-working. But if supporters had thought the bottom had been reached, they were to be disappointed.

Season 1957-58 turned out to be disastrous. Somehow, despite losing successive games 7-0 and 6-0, (the first was the debut game for new signing Charlie Hurley), Sunderland didn't hit rock bottom until March, but there was an inevitability about relegation, even though it went right down to the last Game.

Sunderland finished in 21st place, equal on points with four other teams, but with a far worse goal average. So after 68 years and 57 seasons of Division One football, Sunderland suffered their first ever relegation.

The end of the season also saw the retirement of Len Shackleton. After sustaining an injury in the first game of the campaign, he had never played again and departed Roker Park after setting a post-war club record of 348 appearances, with 101 goals.

There was also disappointment when Don Revie, whom Brown had hoped to build the team around, quickly jumped ship. Daniel, Fleming and Bingham also joined the exodus, and by the end of 1958, only one player major player remained from the top flight era, Stan Anderson, the local lad, who had cost the club the princely sum of his £10 signing on fee.

Alan Brown chats with Don Revie

The team now appeared to be in freefall, and at one stage, it even looked possible that they could slip through the trapdoor into Division Three, but they rallied to finish in an uninspiring 15th place.

The next season followed a similar pattern, run of the mill football, played out by the season's end, in front of only 20,000 dispirited spectators.

Unable to attract the type of quality signings they needed, they were forced to rely more on home grown talent, but the quality just didn't seem to be there, and there seemed to be no way out of this spiral. An air of depression had settled over the club, and this seemed to express itself in the often tepid displays by the players.

It wasn't until an adverse incident away at Anfield that the cloud was lifted, after a clear the air meeting amongst the players, led to an improved run of form.

But it was to be the arrival of one of the area's biggest soccer personalities, that was to lift the gloom, and provide the springboard for a return to the top flight.

CHARLES BUCHAN'S FOOTBALL MONTHLY

Edited by—CHARLES BUCHAN
and JOHN THOMPSON

Associate Editor—J. M. SARL

JUNE, 1957 - - - No. 70

CONTENTS

Published by Charles Buchan's Publications Ltd., 408 Strand, London, W.C.2. Printed in Great Britain by Samuel Stephen Ltd., Upper Norwood, S.E.19. Distributed by Hulton Press Ltd., Hulton House, Fleet Street, London, E.C.4. World Copyright strictly reserved by the Publishers.

CONDITIONS OF SALE AND SUPPLY. This magazine is sold subject to the following conditions, namely, that it shall not, without the written consent of the publishers first given, be lent, re-sold, hired out or otherwise disposed of by way of Trade except at the full retail price of 1s. 6d. (or 2s. general overseas, 2s. 3d. South Africa) and that it shall not be lent, re-sold, hired out or otherwise disposed of in a mutilated condition or in any unauthorised cover by way of Trade; or affixed to or as part of any publication or advertising, literary or pictorial matter whatsoever.

OPINION
by
CHARLES BUCHAN

Former captain of England, Sunderland and Arsenal

SUNDERLAND'S TRAGEDY IS NOT IN VAIN

THE tragedy of the Sunderland Case is that the impression has been given to many of the public that honourable men have been found guilty of a criminal act.

The truth, of course, is that those who have been punished, HAD BROKEN NO LAW OF THE LAND. They had merely disregarded the FOOTBALL LEAGUE'S rules and regulations.

To my mind, the disturbing feature is that they could not appeal to a higher court against the judgment. That is inconsistent with British justice. Surely, they should have been allowed to present their case through legal channels?

All they did was to try and further the interests of their club which they had so much at heart. They were ultra-keen to keep Sunderland—who have been a First Division team since they joined the League in 1890—at the top of the tree.

Most of the Sunderland directors are old friends of mine. They were not in the game in order to make money, but simply because they loved it.

THEY CAN REAP SOME SATISFACTION, HOWEVER, FROM THE FACT THAT THEIR ACTIONS WILL EVENTUALLY BENEFIT PLAYERS AND THE GAME IN GENERAL.

Once the furore and fuss have died down, the League Management Committee must revise their regulations relating to the transfer of players.

It is odd to think that a man, when he is transferred, can receive no more than the £10 signing-on fee and accrued share of benefit, amounting to £150 for every year he has served the club parting with him.

This regulation has been in force for a long time. It may have been appropriate when most transfer fees were in hundreds of pounds, not thousands, as they are at present.

It is hopelessly out of date now.

When the Tribunal, appointed a few years ago to settle the differences between the F.A., the Football League and the Players' Union, gave their findings, they advised the League to introduce a new transfer system.

The official statement by the Joint Commission of the F.A. and Football League announced:

1. Sunderland F.C. have been fined £5,000 and are ordered to pay the cost of the inquiry into their financial affairs.

2. Mr. E. W. Ditchburn, Sunderland F.C. chairman, and Mr. W. S. Martin, director, have been suspended permanently from all football and football management.

3. Mr. S. Ritson (vice-chairman) and Mr. L. W. Evans, both directors of the Sunderland club and members of the Finance Committee, have been suspended sine die.

4. Four other directors, Colonel J. Turnbull, Messrs. S. Collings, J. Reed and J. Parker are severely censured.

5. Players involved in charges of illegal payments by the Sunderland club are to be summoned to a joint enquiry.

6. A decision with regard to the manager, Mr. Bill Murray, and secretary, Mr. George Crow, has been deferred.

They also suggested a way in which the fees should be distributed—among the two clubs concerned, the player, and a common pool to be shared among the rest of the clubs.

In my opinion, it was not a good scheme. But I think it was on the right lines and, with modification, worthy of consideration.

During my early playing days, and after the First World War, a player was entitled to 10 per cent of the fee paid for his transfer. It worked well until the players demanded more.

I SUGGEST THAT A PORTION OF THE FEE, SOMETHING LIKE THAT, WOULD BE AN ADMIRABLE SOLUTION.

It has its loopholes, I know, but it would prevent a recurrence of the Sunderland affair.

Keepers UNDER STRESS!

Willie Fraser watches this effort from Albion's Derek Kevan sail over the bar.

Grainger of Sunderland waits to pounce if Ditchburn of Tottenham makes a mistake.

Is this ballet or football at Goodison Park.

Even this flying leap by Fraser the Sunderland keeper, cannot keep out this long range effort from Ryan the Charlton winger

A SONG IN PRAISE OF SOCCER

by COLIN GRAINGER
Sunderland and England

THEY tell me I'm a mug. Even some of the biggest names in football say I'm a fool for not giving up Soccer and concentrating on singing as a career. They say that, of course, because they know I've received as much as £100 a night for singing a few songs in variety theatres.

And against that a professional footballer's wage is chicken feed.

But always I tell these well-meaning people that the game will always come first in my life. Like everything else, the football business has its faults. But I love it.

I realise that my first breaks in show business came because I had the excellent gimmick of being an England international left-winger. It wasn't until later that my voice alone got me bookings and recording appointments.

I never nurtured any hope of becoming a top singer, but I'd always wished to be a star footballer. It had been my ambition for as long as I could remember and, for that matter, it's still my aim to be a better player.

Ours was a football-minded household in the Yorkshire pit village of Havercroft, seven miles from Wakefield. I got my first pair of football boots and my first football when I was only three.

And I must have just started at Ryhill infants' school when I first graced the Mecca of all the village's aspiring footballers—"The Square".

I was a natural left-footer and generally, I played at inside-left—or thereabouts. And despite my position I still would say, "I'm Stanley Matthews"— a claim which got me into some rows with the rightful occupant of the right-wing berth.

I didn't dream then, of course, that years later my greatest goal would come from a Matthews centre in a Wembley international.

By the time I reached Ryhill and South Hiendley Secondary Modern School the word had got around that I was a useful player, and I was chosen for Green House.

It wasn't long before I got a place in the school team and, aged 11, I was easily the baby of the side when I played

my first game in the South Elmsall and District League.

The match was with Upton Colliery School and I was as proud as Punch as I trotted out. Soon I was even more proud, for I was picked for the League team. For three seasons I played with South Elmsall Boys, and I became a left-winger when I was 14.

But we never won anything; we had only about half a dozen schools to choose from.

In fact, I must have an unusual record among international footballers. I have never won a medal, a Cup replica—not even a badge in any class of football.

I earned the only medal I have by playing cricket!

Came my 15th birthday and "Tal" Grainger—that was my nickname—left school.

My ambition was still to be a professional footballer. But no high-powered manager was waiting at the school gates.

I started an apprenticeship at a small engineering works in Wakefield. While there I played for Ryhill Juniors, an under-18 side, in the Barnsley Intermediate League.

I had worked under a Mr. Hepplethwaite for 12 months when my cousin, Denis Grainger, formerly Leeds United's left-winger, told me he had arranged a pre-season trial for me at his club, Wrexham.

Luckily, I could hardly do a thing wrong on the day and immediately after the game, Leslie McDowall, then Wrexham's manager and now Manchester City's boss, asked me to join the ground staff.

I couldn't say "yes" quick enough.

Dad had gone with me to Wrexham. He went to the works as soon as he got back to Yorkshire and told Mr. Hepplethwaite I had become a footballer.

Mr. Hepplethwaite, and all the men at work, were delighted.

Another thing I'll never forget—Mr. Hepplethwaite sent me an extra week's wage . . . £1 7s 1½d.

I've never regretted switching to full-time football. The Monday after that Saturday trial match was for me the beginning of a great adventure which isn't yet ended.

My League debut wasn't to come until the next season, but I was only 16 when I joined Wrexham and only 17 when I played in my first game, against Hartlepools United.

There's many a joke among footballers about how Servicemen get time off to play football, but I wasn't so lucky. I spent most of my National Service with the R.A.F. in Hampshire, and I managed only half-a-dozen games for Wrexham.

One day I received a telegram from Wrexham's new manager, Peter Jackson. You can imagine my delight when I learned that Sheffield United wanted to sign me, for Sheffield was only 20 miles from my Havercroft home.

When I met Sheffield's manager, Reg Freeman, in a London hotel, he didn't have to ask me twice to sign. I cost Sheffield £2,500.

Just before demob, however, I broke a wrist and it was still in plaster when I played my first League game against Charlton. I should not have played. Far from being a dream debut, it was a nightmare. I had a shocker and spent the next two months in the reserves.

The next season, 1954-55, I had 26 first-team games, but I was really still at the apprentice stage.

But in the close season Joe Mercer arrived as boss. And with his arrival came my success. Under his guidance my play improved considerably.

I owe more to him than anybody in football. I remember him telling me: *"You could be a great player. All you need is confidence in yourself."*

His words worked wonders.

That same season I played for the Football League in Belfast and three days later I learned I'd been chosen as England's left-winger against Brazil, at Wembley.

I had the luck to score after only four minutes. Then midway through the second half came my greatest goal.

I jumped as I'd never jumped before to head in a terrific centre from Stanley Matthews. We won 4—2. And that was the first of seven caps to come my way.

Finally, those inspiring words of advice from Joe Mercer earned his club £17,000 and a right-winger, Sam Kemp, when I moved to Sunderland.

CHARLIE HURLEY

Sunderland

I was picked for Eire and all set for my first big chance, and then it happened . . .

I SUPPOSE everyone can recall a moment when the bottom dropped out of their world. I certainly can remember mine.

I was selected for the Republic of Ireland team to play Spain. It was the thrill of a life-time, but I never played in that match. It was a Sunday game, and on the previous Wednesday I turned out for my battalion team at Aldershot.

Towards the end of the match, I twisted my knee. It happened simply

INJURED
for 15 months!

enough, just through jumping over an opponent who had sprawled in front of me. I was carried off and taken to hospital.

I can't attempt to describe the dejection I felt. I was out of the Eire team, and also out of Millwall's side. And it was fifteen months before my knee was really normal again, although I had returned to active football long before that time.

I hope I never have such a worrying time again. Often during those months I wondered how much my football career was in danger.

Nevertheless, I certainly did everything I could to hasten my recovery, even to buying a set of weight-lifting apparatus. By regular exercises I was able to build up the leg muscles affected by the injury.

That taught me the value of weight-lifting as an aid to physical fitness. I still include it in my training schedule, and thoroughly recommend it to all young players.

But though that injury at Aldershot cost me an international cap, I did get a souvenir of the game in the shape of a letter of sympathy from Johnny Carey, the Blackburn Rovers manager, who looked after the Eire team.

I appreciated that letter, and will always keep it.

Then, last May, opportunity knocked once more, and this time everything came right. I played against England at Dalymount Park, Dublin, in the World Cup Qualifying Competition.

We drew 1—1, and I had the job of marking Manchester United's Tommy Taylor. What a player he is! A bundle of energy, he is just the type to keep a centre-half on tenterhooks.

Tommy ranks high as a centre-forward,

but I had already met some as lively while I was playing for Millwall in the Third Division. One of the most difficult to deal with was Tommy Johnston of Leyton Orient.

When Orient won promotion to the Second Division, I was relieved—to know I should be missing him !

I was born in Cork, but came to England when I was ten, and never trod the soil of Southern Ireland again until that international match last May.

My parents settled at Rainham, in Essex, and that's where I was brought up.

As a small boy, I was keen on both football and running. I kicked a ball about whenever and wherever I could but the first proper match I played in was for Blacksmith's Lane School, Rainham. I was captain and outside-right. And, believe it or not, I played in slippers and ordinary socks !

I had a football shirt and shorts, but not the rest of the outfit. When I managed to buy a pair of black football boots soon after, my feet felt in clover.

I had left school, and was playing for the Rainham Youth Centre when Millwall spotted me.

We were playing in the final of the Andrews Cup. Our opponents were the Woodford Youth Centre, and the match was on the Woodford Town ground.

Bill Voisey, who has discovered many players for Millwall, was there to watch the Woodford centre-forward.

We lost 1—0, and I felt very disappointed as I dressed after the game. Then Bill came in to introduce himself. It seemed he had become more interested in me than the Woodford player.

He said he would call at my home and

in due course along he came, together with Ron Gray, now Millwall's manager.

I signed amateur forms, and when the next season came round, I was given a game in the reserve team at Fulham and I felt so nervous before the game, I couldn't even talk !

I did nothing spectacular, but was quite pleased with my display, and Charlie Hewitt, then managing Millwall, offered me a ground-staff job.

I preferred to carry on with my work as an apprenticed toolmaker, but told him I would be willing to turn professional when I was 17.

That's how it worked out, and I stayed with Millwall until my transfer to Sunderland in the last week of September.

But it might so easily have been different, for there was a time when I was wearing the West Ham colours.

Wally St. Pier, their chief scout, approached me while I was playing for the Rainham Youth Centre and asked me to play for West Ham's colts team. Then Ted Fenton, West Ham's manager, offered me a job on the ground staff, but as I was better off at my toolmaking job, I declined.

Kichenbrand takes a crack at the ball and Queen of the South goal-keeper Henderson was knocked on the head, but soon recovered.

by DON KICHENBRAND

Sunderland

MY REPLY TO MY CRITICS

I HAVE made three soccer resolutions since I came to Britain from South Africa in September, 1955.

1, TO AVERAGE A GOAL A GAME.

That I decided, would be my duty as Rangers' centre-forward shortly after I got into the first team. That was my New Year Resolution for 1956. By the end of the 1955-1956 season, I had accomplished it. I had played in 28 games and scored 28 goals.

2, TO BECOME A MASTER OF THE ART OF BALL CONTROL.

This is most difficult. It will take a lot of practice, with ball work all the time. But it's something I'm really concentrating on this season. I hope to get it to a fine art one day. That's why I've decided . . .

3, TO BELIEVE THAT PATIENCE IS THE GREATEST VIRTUE.

One of the things that taught me to believe in that maxim was the spell I had in hospital at the start of season 1956-1957 when I had my appendix removed.

Most players dread injury—and I don't say I enjoy it! But some worry when they're injured. They're scared of losing their places. But most of all they seem to give themselves ulcers about the TIME that they're losing. Especially with long injuries.

I don't believe in rushing things. I think you must let nature take its course. That period in hospital helped to teach me that.

As I say, I feel that time is on my side —I'm only 24—and that I can become more of an all-round footballer. That is my reply to the criticism that *I am too robust . . . that I bulldoze instead of ballplay.*

Well, I just play my natural game. Perhaps I have been trying too much. Perhaps I am too keen.

But I firmly believe that if I keep trying all the time I am bound to profit by an opponent's slip.

I feel that I cannot change my style . . . *but I can improve it.*

And that as I say, is what I aim to do.

That's why I am doing all I can to master ball control. At first, this may slow me down a bit. Time alone will allow me to ally the control I gain to the speed I've got.

Only then will I be happy with my play.

I had few critics among the large and wonderful Rangers following. I am hoping that I shall be equally happy with the keen Sunderland supporters at Roker Park.

I signed for Sunderland just before 'dead-line' day on March 16.

It always comforts me to know the crowd are behind me.

Referring to criticism, from others, of my style. I've been playing the same game since I came here and it's only recently that a few differences have crept in.

" I'm sorry I shouted you were an old woman ! "

I know I am improving. I feel my ball control is better.

I was able to compare my old self with my new self when I went to South Africa during the last close season for a holiday.

In 1954, when Stanley Matthews visited the Union, I played alongside him. I found my poor Soccer brain wasn't thinking with him at all. I was away behind.

In the summer of 1957, I again played in a South African match with the Old Master . . . and I scored four goals. We were in the forward line of a team called the ex-Professionals, against a South African XI. We beat them 7—3.

So in those three years, I had gained the experience needed to play along-side the Master Craftsman Matthews.

In one of those ex-Pros. v. Amateurs matches—I was playing for the Amateurs before I came to Britain—I got my biggest total of goals. I scored five in our 6—3 win.

That was the game in which Charlie Watkins (ex-Rangers) saw me—he was left-half for the ex-Pros. He asked me if I was interested in going to Britain. Having just completed my apprenticeship as an engineer — I finished my time in August, 1955 — I said "yes."

I had been asked by Hearts, on their 1954 tour of South Africa, if I would like to join them, but my father insisted that I should serve my time.

That year I was top goal-scorer in the League with 24 goals, including six hat-tricks.

Before I had been a whole season with Rangers I'd beaten that total.

I had also equalled my highest score of five goals against Queen of the South when we beat them 8—0, at Ibrox on our last run in to win the League Championship flag of 1955-1956.

THE COD-LIVER OIL KID

That's what they call me says

ALAN O'NEILL, Sunderland

I AM one of the few, one of the VERY few North-Eastern born players in post-war years to play regularly for Sunderland before last season.

But you watch—most of Sunderland's first-team players of tomorrow will have Geordie accents. And I like to think that we young Sunderland players—or the "Brown Bairns" as we are sometimes called—will be a force to be reckoned with in a couple of seasons.

Like many of my younger colleagues, I owe a lot to manager Alan Brown and others. But I owe most to my grandmother, Mrs. Mary Graham, with whom I still live near the riverside in Sunderland.

But for her I wouldn't have been able to play football for anybody. When I was seven I was desperately ill with pleurisy. To make matters worse, the Deptford area around our house was being bombed night after night and I had to be carried to and from the air-raid shelter.

My Grandma says that several times they thought they were going to lose me.

Friends tell me that my grandmother nursed me with as much skill and devotion as a qualified nurse, and after a month my recovery started.

Then came her building-up recipe—cod-liver oil and malt. Three times a day I was made to take a table-spoonful and I was able to return to school four months later.

Even now my daily dose is two tablespoonfuls of cod-liver oil from a huge jar. No wonder the other players at Roker Park sometimes call me the Cod-Liver Oil Kid!

I wasn't interested in football until I was nine. In Soccer-mad Sunderland, even babies in cradles are supposed to kick with the in-step. And as I was born in the year when Sunderland won the F.A. Cup for the only time in their history, I probably seemed a strange lad to the neighbours.

Then schoolmaster Ernest Armstrong saw me kicking a ball around with a few of the lads, and he put me in the school juniors' team the next Saturday.

I still wasn't sufficiently interested to get a pair of proper football boots. But after I'd played only two or three games I was chosen for a representative trial match, so my grandfather bought me a pair of boots.

Then the Soccer bug really got hold of me. For not only was I chosen to play for the town's junior schools —I was made captain, too.

I went straight into the second team when I moved to secondary modern school. But then I thought the world had come to an end—*I was dropped because Mr. Gibson, the sportsmaster, said I was far too selfish with the ball.*

I was heartbroken, and when I got back to the side a week later I had learned a lesson. And I was never dropped again from that side, the school first team or Sunderland Boys for whom I played the next season.

By this time, of course, the lad who'd been so dis-

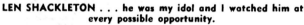

LEN SHACKLETON . . . he was my idol and I watched him at every possible opportunity.

RAICH CARTER . . . one of Sunderland's greatest local boys who made good.

interested in football was mad about it. After I'd played in the morning, I'd be at Roker Park, cheering Sunderland, idolising Len Shackleton and piling up a huge collection of autographs.

I still have at home autographed copies of Charles Buchan's Football Monthly.

So you can imagine my delight when on leaving school I was invited by manager Bill Murray to become a Sunderland amateur. I was to have moved to Morecambe where my parents have a taxi business, but they let me stay on Wearside where I became an apprentice painter and decorator.

Twice I wanted to quit Roker Park as a 16-year-old because I thought I wasn't getting enough games. In fact, once I asked the club to cancel my registration so that I could go to Huddersfield. But I'm glad I was persuaded to change my mind.

For Sunderland are a great club. We younger players had a wonderful time in the 1955-56 season, the first season of the Northern Intermediate League, an under-18 competition for League clubs in the North. We won the League championship and the Cup.

Several of that side are still Sunderland players and three of them—goalkeeper Ronnie Routledge, full-back Allen Graham and wing-half Graham Reed, played for Sunderland's first team last season.

That year with the juniors was a very important one in my Soccer apprenticeship and, on the day after my 19th birthday, came perhaps my most important

game. It certainly earned me a first-team place.

It was an under-23 charity game at Roker Park between Sunderland and Newcastle. A 2—2 draw, it was hailed by many critics as one of the best exhibitions of Soccer seen there.

The next day I learned that I was to play for the senior side at Cardiff. I almost danced with joy when I was told the news.

My first thought was to ring my parents at Morecambe, I must have asked for Morecambe 2826 dozens of times that night, but unfortunately there was a fault on the line and I couldn't get through.

They heard of my selection the next day. Dad, who is mad on football, was delighted. It was as a sign of gratitude to my stepfather that I changed my name from Hope to O'Neill last close season.

That game at Cardiff was Don Revie's first for Sunderland and though he wasn't quite back to top fitness after injury, he still showed sufficient classical touches to make me realise he was a great player.

Soon, one Soccer reporter described me as the best home-produced Sunderland inside-forward prospect since Raich Carter. That meant little to me, of course, for I never saw Raich play. But I've heard all about Raich and my ambition is not to disappoint that reporter who compared me with him.

For if I achieved anything like Carter's prowess, it would do Sunderland a lot of good. And Sunderland's return to the top is my greatest wish.

JACK OF ALL TRADES

but it's best to be master of one

JACK of all trades and master of none! Is that the fate of too many players these days? I must admit I thought so at one stage of my career with Luton Town. So badly did I feel about being switched from one position to another that I asked for a move.

But the Luton board turned down my request—and I was very glad! For the next week I was tried in another strange berth—left-half—for a visit to Leeds.

That switch was the turning-point in my career.

I faced the great John Charles, but I had a good game and we beat Leeds 2—1. From that match until the time I left Luton, the left-half position was mine.

After four eventful seasons with Luton, during which time I had representative honours for the Football League v. The Irish League at Leeds (my lucky ground) and for an F.A. XI v. The Army, at Manchester, I was transferred to Sunderland.

The Wearsiders had been interested in me for a long time, and they came to terms with Luton last February.

Shortly after joining Sunderland, I was again honoured by the Football League against the Scottish League, at Newcastle. After that appearance my thoughts centred on the possibility of earning a full cap. So far, I am unlucky.

Another disappointment was the relegation of Sunderland, at the end of last season, to the Second Division for the first time.

Like most boys who played the

"It must be something serious, doctor—he's decided not to go to football!"

by REG PEARCE
Sunderland

game, I always wanted to be a professional footballer. But, unlike most, I was lucky enough to achieve my ambition.

I was only twelve when I started playing for my local Boys Brigade team in the Liverpool area. I represented my Battalion against Southport, Birkenhead and Manchester.

Then I joined Old Swan Boys Club, in a higher grade of football.

After a few more seasons in local amateur leagues, I signed amateur forms for Liverpool and for two seasons played in the 'A' and 'B' teams at Anfield.

But I did not seem to make much progress, and I eventually joined the well-known northern amateur club, Marine F.C., in the Lancashire Combination.

In my two seasons with Marine I had county honours for Liverpool and Lancashire. During one of these inter-county matches I played alongside Bill Slater, the Wolves and England left-half—little realising that one day I would play against him in top-class football.

On leaving Marine, I joined Winsford United, in the Cheshire League, as a part-time professional. After playing for them for about two months, fortune smiled on me.

George Martin, then chief scout of Luton Town, had been watching me, and I signed full-time professional forms for them in late November, 1954.

This was a most important step for me to take, as it meant giving up my trade and leaving home. But I certainly do not regret the move.

As you may guess, I was a little bewildered by the sudden change in my day-to-day life, but I soon settled down to the serious business of professional football.

I completed the rest of the 1954-55 season in Luton reserves, at inside-right.

Two events stand out from my first season at Kenilworth Road—Luton's promotion to Division I for the first time, and my one game in the first team at outside-right, against West Ham.

Strangely enough, my first outing as a First Division player was at outside-right, against Spurs.

I have played in many grand games and one that stands out in my memory is an evening game with Wolves.

I was playing inside-left. We were 2—0 up in ten minutes; losing 2—3 after half-an-hour, and at half-time 3—5 down. In the second half we managed to pull a goal back, making it 4—5.

Minutes from the end, I headed the ball from a corner against the bar, only to see it rebound into play. The final score was 5—4 for the Wolves. But what a game!

The crowd cheered us off the field. It is still said that it was one of the best League games seen at Molineux for a long time.

It was also a personal triumph for our inside-right, Gordon Turner, who scored a hat-trick.

I was glad it turned out such an exciting game, as my father had travelled from Liverpool—the first time he had seen me play professionally.

Since being at Sunderland I have been greatly impressed with the modern facilities there — all that a footballer could wish for.

Sunderland are a club of great tradition and I sincerely hope that by the end of this season we are back in Division I.

My career so far has brought me in contact with many sporting personalities, and the many different countries I have visited on tour are only a few of the pleasures one can get out of football.

It's a great life, a grand profession, and I strongly recommend it to any boy wishing to take up the game seriously.

CHARLIE
HURLEY
Sunderland

AN ADVERTISEMENT STARTED IT ALL

by PETER WAKEHAM
Sunderland

A SMALL advertisement in a local newspaper in 1952 brought me into big football. In the advert.—which I read quite casually — Mr. Eric Webber, then the Torquay United player-manager, stated that he intended to form a youth team at Plainmoor and invited applications from local youngsters for trials.

I was just 16 and had been playing in goal for my native Kingsbridge, which lies between Torquay and Plymouth.

Anyway, I went to the Torquay ground, played in an early season trial and was invited to sign amateur forms. For about a season I appeared in Torquay's third team in a local League.

I was a clerk in the Kingsbridge Council offices in those days, but when I became 17 I was asked to sign as a full-time professional at Plainmoor—and so started a career of which I had never dreamed.

That was in the 1953-54 season, and I spent that winter in the second string, learning all the time.

On Easter Monday, 1954, Mr. Webber decided that I was ready for my League team 'blooding', and I went into the side against Newport County.

We won 3—2, but I can't remember much about my contribution. I was supposed to play in the rest of the Easter games, but I developed a troublesome throat infection and could not turn out again that season.

During the summer, I went into the Army and my chance of playing for Torquay the following winter was limited.

At Aldershot, where I was stationed, I played a lot of Soccer in company with Charlie Hurley, of Millwall, now a Roker Park colleague of mine.

And I was also fortunate to meet the girl who is now my wife.

While I was away on National Service, Torquay signed big Alf Jeffries from Brentford, and when I got home I had to be content with reserve games.

But at the end of the 1955-56 season I appeared in a few first-team matches for Torquay, and was demobbed from the Army in the following summer.

That enabled me to start the next season in full-time training, and I began as first-team goalkeeper.

But luck was not with me, for after a dozen matches I dislocated an elbow at Shrewsbury by falling awkwardly on a hard ground.

For a goalkeeper this is a serious injury. I was out of action for nearly two months and I didn't feel too confident when I began playing again. In fact, I was unable to gain my League place.

The 1957-58 season brought better fortune—at first. I began confidently in the first team and, in the October, played for the F.A. against the R.A.F. at Nottingham.

We won that game 5—2 and the following Wednesday I was reserve to Alan Hodgkinson in the England Under-23 team against Rumania.

Then came another serious blow to my ambitions. When playing at Brighton, in December, I broke a wrist and was out of the game for another long spell.

But by the Easter I was back in the team—and I regained my old confidence right away.

Then came a momentous period—but not before injury had hit me again.

Last season, after three games, I was kicked in the back and was unfit for our next match.

The mid-week games were still running, and our reserve goalkeeper, Mervyn Gill, came in to replace me.

Well, it happened! Mervyn—a very good goalkeeper—played the proverbial 'blinder', and I couldn't get back.

I was beginning to think that my career was to be ruined by these injuries, when one day Eric Webber told me that Sunderland were showing signs of interest in me.

The next Saturday they came to watch me in a reserve game.

On the same day Mervyn Gill was injured in the first-team match, and on the next Monday, Sunderland's manager Alan Brown watched me play for the first team.

When I reported the next day for training, Mr. Webber took me into his office and introduced me to Mr. Brown.

He told me that he was trying to build a young team which would take Sunderland back to the First Division, and would I like to go to Roker Park as part of his long-term plan?

I was happy enough at Torquay, and the north-east seemed bleak and far away. But I was anxious to get on, and it was too good an opportunity to miss.

So I went.

I had a few games in North Eastern League Soccer with Sunderland's reserves, but on the first day of last November, I was called on to make my Second Division debut in place of Johnny Bollands, against Grimsby.

That match was at Roker Park and we won 1—0, so that I had the great satisfaction of keeping my goal intact in that first, testing game in front of the critical Sunderland fans.

I felt happy with my display and I retained my League place for the rest of last season.

'When I went in to the First Division . . . I felt like a man who sells his pre-war second-hand car and starts to drive the latest power model without experience . . . but

NOW I AM IN GEAR ON THE WEAR'

by
CHARLES HURLEY
Sunderland

THIRTEEN goals against us in two games—and I was the centre-half! That was the debut I had to endure with Sunderland in the autumn of 1957. No wonder I wished I was back again in good old London.

And when I say that at the time I hadn't really wanted to leave London for the north-east, you can imagine how terrible I felt during my first few days as a First Division footballer.

I had been capped twice for my native Eire when Sunderland first came after me, but I did not want to go so far away from my home in London.

I had just about recovered from a serious cartilage injury which had kept me out of active Soccer for the best part of 15 months, and was rapidly regaining my best form with Millwall.

Then, one Wednesday morning, Ron Gray, the Millwall manager, came on to the pitch where I was training and told me that Alan Brown, the Sunderland manager, was at the ground and wanted to see me.

I told Mr. Gray that he was wasting his time and that I was set against going to Wearside. There didn't seem much point in discussing the matter further as far as I was concerned.

But Mr. Gray persuaded me at least to see the Sunderland chief, who had travelled such a long way.

I have to hand it to Mr. Brown for his persistence which in the end got him his man.

But he didn't catch me until we had talked for more than two hours and he had taken me to lunch and come round to my house that evening for another long discussion about my future.

Later that night I agreed to join Sunderland, although I was still very doubtful and felt in my heart of hearts that I should have said 'No'.

What decided me was the knowledge that I had to further my Soccer career. And I knew that Sunderland were a good club to play for, although they already looked booked for a struggle to avoid relegation.

I was courting at the time, and the girl who is now my wife sent me a good luck telegram which cheered me up no end. Ours was a strange courtship after that, for I saw her only about once every two weeks when I moved north.

My first game for Sunderland was at Blackpool, and I started my First Division match full of hope. What a disaster that game proved to be!

We were thrashed 7—0. I couldn't do a thing right, and Ray Charnley, who had only just come into the Blackpool team at centre-forward, got two goals.

I realised afterwards that I could not play worse if I tried, and I resolved to do a lot better in the next game, which was also an away fixture—at Burnley.

Alas for my optimism! We were beaten 6—0. But at least I had the satisfaction of preventing Burnley's young leader, Ray Pointer, from scoring.

My first home game was against Preston, and I wondered just how the Roker Park crowd would take to an expensive new centre-half who had cost their club something like £18,000 and who had so far failed miserably to plug a defence that was leaking like a colander.

But we did a lot better against Preston, and I had a fine reception from our supporters.

I remember that a newspaper kidded me into writing an article after the Burnley defeat. It was to appear the day after my home debut.

When I arrived at Roker Park I was confronted with bills plastered everywhere, carrying my photograph and bearing the words in huge type: 'I'm no flop, says Charlie Hurley'.

Well, I was determined to prove that I was no flop, and since those two 'Best forgotten' games I think I have managed to do so.

When I went into the First Division from the Third, I felt rather like a man who sells his old pre-war second-hand car and starts to drive the latest power model without experience.

Everything seemed far too fast. I often felt the game was running away with me, and yet when I got on the ball it appeared that I had more time and room to do something with it.

That was because of the extra brain and class in the First Division, compared with the Third.

As I am by nature a constructive player, the new style of play demanded of me suited me ideally—once I had found my feet.

Unfortunately, Sunderland were relegated for the first time in their history at the end of my first season at Roker.

On the last day of the season we were at Portsmouth while Leicester City, our companions in distress, were at Birmingham. Sheffield Wednesday were already doomed to relegation.

The position was that Portsmouth and Newcastle, just above us, were almost safe with superior goal records, and that Leicester also had a better average than us.

We had the same number of points, but while Sunderland had to win by a big score, Leicester could get by on a single goal.

And that is what happened in Leicester's game. Our kick-off at Fratton Park was 15 minutes earlier than that at Birmingham and, after we had licked Pompey 2—0, we sat and waited in the bath for the Leicester result to come through.

When we heard that Leicester had won 1—0 (a surprise result on form) we knew we were down. But the Sunderland players and officials took it amazingly well.

Going back north in the train that night, we all resolved to do our utmost to help the grand old club back to their rightful place in the First Division.

It is easy to talk, of course, and as I write we have still to get back. In fact, at one stage in our opening campaign in the Second Division we were lying second from the bottom of the table, and there were fears that we might do what Derby County did and slip right through to the Third Division.

I am very happy at Sunderland now. I could not have been treated better by any other club, and now my wife and I have just moved into a nice club house at Roker, not far from the sea.

By the way, I'm hoping that another Hurley may soon make a name for himself as a professional. He is my younger brother, Arthur, a tall, wiry type of inside-forward, who recently signed amateur forms for my old club, Millwall.

PETER WAKEHAM

LEN ASHURST

COLIN NELSON

AMBROSE FOGARTY

SUNDERLAND

COLIN GRAINGER

STAN ANDERSON

Not being much of a prophet, I can't say what football has in store for me.

Something I can say, it has been great being captain of Sunderland, especially over the past 12 months.

After two months of the 1960-61 season the team didn't seem to be getting anywhere. We started reasonably well, then came a bad spell that meant eleven games without a win.

Depression on Wearside. Nobody wanted to know us. The silver lining had to come from behind the cloud and never was one more welcome. We started to win instead of losing.

When that sort of thing happens, it can usually be traced to one factor. Sometimes the signing of a new player, sometimes a change in tactics. Something quite different started Sunderland's revival, brought the crowds rolling back and made First Division football look like returning to Roker Park.

This all-important factor was a penalty kick. It was given against us when we played Liverpool at Anfield last October. It was a tough decision…on Sunderland.

As we saw the incident, Jimmy McNab took the ball from Liverpool inside-right Roger Hunt quite fairly. Roger certainly fell inside our penalty-area, but the tackle took place a yard outside.

To our amazement, the referee consulted a linesman and then pointed to the spot. Jimmy Harrower took the kick and scored.

When Liverpool score a goal, the Anfield crowd really let themselves go. Not this time, a half-hearted cheer clearly showed that they didn't think much of the penalty award either.

As we took up our position to kick off, I thought 'here we go again.' Sunderland were really in the depths, we hadn't been playing well and didn't have to be told that our last win was ten games back. In that mood a goal against us meant tails down. The reaction in the team after that goal was TAILS UP!

I could feel it. The goal, instead of starting up the usual depression, turned us into fighters. I can't explain it, but the mood completely changed. We equalised soon afterwards and held Liverpool, going strongly at that time, to a draw.

We headed to the tunnel feeling we had done a good job and really enjoyed our bath. Our dressing-room was the cheeriest place I'd been in for weeks. After all, we had finished level with a team strongly fancied for promotion. We got talking on the way back to Sunderland. Where had we been going wrong? Why had we fought back when so often we had just folded up and been beaten.

These questions and a lot of others were all given a good going over as the train dashed along. Little points in play, which didn't appear to have much importance at the time, were analysed. Before we reached Sunderland everything had been ironed out and it was resolved we should go all out to be a better team.

Looking back on that train journey, I think we psycho-analysed ourselves out of a very deep depression. Maybe we had come to the end of a bad run in the natural way of things, but that talking session, sparked off by the penalty that never was, must have helped.

The very next week a new spirit developed at Roker Park, I can't put the difference down in cold print, but I could feel it. For one thing, my job as captain became easier.

During our bad run, I would speak to another

AS SHOWN ON I.T.V.

SUBBUTEO Regd
TABLE SOCCER

THE
REPLICA
OF
ASSOCIATION
FOOTBALL

COMPLETE with goals, balls, etc., and teams available in all League club colours.

Here is a game where victory or defeat depends upon the skill of the player with FINGER TIP CONTROL.

22 miniature figures dribble, tackle, crack in goals, dive and save them . . . and are always at your command to produce all the thrills of real league cup and international football.

PRICES: 9/11d., 19/7d., 47/3d.

SUBBUTEO 'TABLE CRICKET'	SUBBUTEO 'TABLE RUGBY'
The replica of Test and County Cricket. Played with teams of Miniature men, ball and stumps with bails. Unique bowling and batting devices. Overarm bowling, double wickets, and all the 'outs' such as clean bowled, stumped, caught, etc. Bodyline bowling, hits for six, four and odd runs.	The replica of Rugby Football. Played with fifteen figures a side. Rugby goals and ball, kicks for touch, runs for the goal-lines, tackles and tries, converted tries and penalty goals as in real Rugby.
PRICES: 9/11d., 14/-, 40/10d.	PRICES: 17/6d. and 37/11d.

Prices post free, or write for full details and order form to:

SUBBUTEO (DEPT. 49) LANGTON GREEN, TUNBRIDGE WELLS, KENT.

SOMETHING TO LIFT US OUT DEPRESSION'

N ANDERSON

DERLAND and ENGLAND

STAN ANDERSON

player during the game and tell him about a mistake he was making. Usually all I got in reply was a sour kind of look. The other player knew where he was going wrong, but he was having a bad time. So were we all, including me.

When the depression lifted, the reaction was so different. When I had to hand out advice I got a cheery, "Okay Stan" in reply.

We became more 'together' than at any time I can remember in nearly twelve years at the club. Moreso even than w hen great players such as George Aitken, Len Shackleton, Ray Daniel and Trevor Ford were in the team. Of course they never had to suffer as the Sunderland team did in the early part of last season.

And talking of last season, something happened that seemed unbelievable to me…. We won three successive away games!

First, we won by the only goal at Sheffield United, then we beat Lincoln City and then we beat Liverpool 2-0 in the Cup.

Before that Liverpool win, of course came the greatest moment Sunderland had experienced for a long time. We beat Arsenal in the third round of the FA Cup.

It turned out to be a great day for yours truly as first, I equalised the score and then scored the winner. This was like old times, a great crowd, fully 58,000, but more importantly the fans saw that we deserved to win and worth coming back to watch.

After the Arsenal game, we went to Liverpool in the fourth round and Norwich in the fifth. We won at both places. Then came the cup-tie that put Sunderland right at the top of the page. We were drawn to play Spurs at Roker Park. Some people fancied our chances, others just couldn't see a Second Division team having

any chance. As for the result, I still think we were unlucky not to win. Spurs did not impress me that day as being the outstanding team they eventually proved themselves to be.

Anyway it ended 1-1 at Roker Park, before Spurs beat us 5-0 in the replay. But we came off the pitch at White Hart Lane feeling far from disgraced. We had two early scoring chances, but missed both, then Spurs scored three in 20 minutes.

Altogether, last season was a red letter one for me. I think I will remember it in greater detail than any other, no matter how long I am with Sunderland, but it still gives me something of a shock to think I might have left the club half-way through.

After a lot of thought, I had requested a transfer. The idea of leaving the club I had joined after leaving school was not a pleasant one. However I thought at the time it was best for both parties. I wasn't playing well and worrying about it. Believe me, I was having my share of the depression that was on at the time.

How glad I am now that nothing developed. It was really something captaining Sunderland in these wonderful months.

ROKER ROARS ITS APPRECIATION

The Charles Buchan's camera was on hand to capture the moment when Sunderland stunned the mighty 'Spurs' in the F.A. Cup, as Willie McPheat equalises for the home team.

Ian McColl

By the May of 1961, the whole of North East football was in the doldrums as Newcastle United had just been relegated to join Sunderland and Middlesbrough in Division Two.

Middlesbrough had a star player though, Brian Clough, and it was common knowledge that he was looking to leave. The centre-forward had endured a fractious relationship with his fellow players for years over his apparent selfishness. His reputation looked to have put off a lot of clubs, although Arsenal were rumoured to be interested, but Alan Brown thought he could handle him.

Brian Clough had been told of Sunderland's interest before he set off on a holiday cruise with his family. He was still undecided on his return, but was finally swayed when he was met by Alan Brown as he disembarked, after the manager had driven all the way down to Southampton to meet him.

It took a £42,000 transfer fee to make the deal happen, a figure that the club couldn't really afford. Eyebrows were also raised that the player hadn't made the jump to Division One football, after all, he was considered to be in almost the same class as Jimmy Greaves, but the promise of £40 per week, and the chance to play in front of 40,000 every week, had clinched the deal.

Clough was not the only major signing made in that period, as it looked as if the 'Bank of England' spending days had returned. Big money was paid to bring in George Herd from Clyde and Harry Hooper from Birmingham City.

Initially it all looked so promising. By October the team was handily placed in the top four, with only their poor away form likely to hamper a promotion push, and after a seven game winning streak, Sunderland went into the final game of the season with destiny firmly in their own hands.

Level on points with Leyton Orient, and with a far better goal average, they just needed to beat Swansea to go up, but despite taking an early lead through Brian Clough, nerves took over and they played out a 1-1 draw whilst Orient were beating Bury.

That campaign might have ended in heartbreak, but worse was to come the following season, as not only were they to finish third once more, missing out on promotion by goal difference, but they were to lose the talismanic Brian Clough, with what turned out to be a career ending injury.

The season was ultra competitive, as six clubs fought out a close battle at the top. After a slow start, Clough was on fire, netting 24 goals in only 20 appearances before the Boxing Day encounter with Bury. Britain was just entering a period of the worst winter weather for years, although initially the North East looked as if it might avoid it, and after a morning pitch inspection, the referee gave the go-ahead for the afternoon's game.

Just before kick-off, the heavens opened, and the resulting snow, hailstones and rain turned the pitch into a quagmire. As Clough chased a through ball from Len Ashurst, there was only one thing on his mind, so he wasn't braced for the sickening collision with Bury keeper Chris Harker. There might have been blood weeping from a head wound, but it was the cruciate ligament damage he suffered, that was to have a devastating impact on the player's career.

Despite this, the other players stepped up, and the season was not de-railed. In particular new signings Johnny Crossan and George Mulhall were superb, so once more Sunderland knew that at least a draw in the final home game to Chelsea, their closest rivals, would have been enough. Alas, despite dominating, they went down to a fluky Chelsea winner, and finished third once more.

These near misses might have crushed the spirit of the team, but it is to their credit that they came back next season and got the job done, all this despite a further bombshell!

Club captain Stan Anderson was considered by supporters to be indispensible. One of the few players to remain after relegation, he was considered to be the heartbeat of the team, but after being replaced by Martin Harvey, he was ushered out of the door with the undue haste, turning up at the press conference called by Newcastle United to announce his signing, with the face of someone attending a funeral. After 14 years and a club record 447 appearances the living embodiment of the team was gone.

Meanwhile, Johnny Crossan and Nick Sharkey, proved up to the task of replacing Clough's goals, with 41 goals between them. However, it was to be the defence, brilliantly marshalled by Charley Hurley, that proved key, as they only conceded 37 goals. The back five remained virtually unchanged throughout. Keeper Jim Montgomery, full backs Len Ashurst and Cec

Roker fans shocked as corner-kick finds net after 26 minutes

TAMBLING SHOOTS CHELSEA INTO LEAD

By L. O. HETHERINGTON

ALTHOUGH queues formed overnight, it was possible to enter Roker Park in comparative comfort shortly before the kick off today when Sunderland met Chelsea in the promotion-or-bust match which rang down the curtain on Wearside soccer for another season.

It was obvious that the gate would be in the region of 60,000 when the teams turned out. This was indeed, Decision Day for Sunderland, who needed a point to ensure First Division football at Roker Park next season after a lapse of five years.

Sunderland stuck to the team which won at Swansea and Luton. Chelsea fielded a shock forward line for a

First-class Scoreboard

KIDS

SOCCER

Hey. Do you mind

Irwin, with Jimmy McNab alongside Hurley.

So after six long years, the wait was over, but just as Sunderland supporters thought they could look ahead with optimism, they were hit once more...with the news that the manager had sensationally walked out, to join Sheffield Wednesday. It didn't even appear to be a football related matter that caused the split, but a disagreement between the manager and the board, as they refused Brown permission to buy his club house!

The first season back in the top flight began in remarkable fashion, as the board decided to manage team affairs themselves, with the help of Charlie Hurley, whilst looking for a new boss. It was during this period, that Brian Clough finally made his First Division debut, scoring his one and only top-flight goal in the process, before bowing to the inevitable and announcing his retirement.

The manager situation couldn't continue, as the club sailed along rudderless, destined for a return to Division Two. The board eventually turned to George Hardwick, who steadied the ship with a couple of astute signings, but also alienated a section of supporters by selling the popular Johnny Crossan to Manchester City.

The tenure of Hardwick was not destined to be a long one, as he was dismissed during the close season, for what he says was his support of Brian Clough, who while still on the payroll, was put in charge of the youth team, despite the directors wanting him out of the club.

The new man in charge was to be Scotland boss Ian McColl, and he was immediately given the

funds to improve the team, returning north of the border and coming back with Neil Martin, and the hopefully sensational Jim Baxter. On his day, Baxter was a masterful footballer, but he also had his demons, mostly to be found in a bottle. It didn't help the player's cause that skipper Charlie Hurley, although recognising the player's skills, didn't like him, or his attitude. Charlie had taken over as Mr Sunderland in supporters' eyes, and wouldn't tolerate any player not putting in 100%.

So despite the genuine talent at the club, it turned out to be another missed opportunity, and as in the early 1950's, there were lowly finishes, 18th and 17th, and as crowds began to decline once more, it looked as if tricky times might be on the horizon.

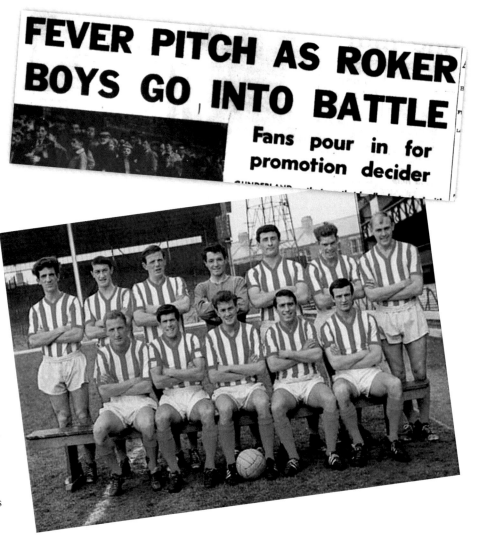

FEVER PITCH AS ROKER BOYS GO INTO BATTLE

Fans pour in for promotion decider

BRIAN CLOUGH
FOR ENGLAND?

LEN
ASHURST
Sunderland

Charles Buchan's

FOOTBALL
MONTHLY

JULY 1961
1/6
Overseas price 2/-
Forces overseas 1/6

STAN ANDERSON
Sunderland

UPS and DOWNS

by LEN ASHURST, Sunderland

HOW quickly depression and elation follow in Soccer! I am thinking of last March when, inside 48 hours, I was transported from elation to deep depression, and back to elation again.

As left-back in the Sunderland team which met Tottenham Hotspur in our sixth round F.A. Cup replay at White Hart Lane, I was excited to think that I was taking part in a game that had captured public imagination, and hopeful that we would beat the Spurs and win a place in the semi-final—even get to Wembley!

Alas for my day dreams! Spurs really rose to the occasion in that replay, when 60,000 of their delirious fans (thousands more were locked out of the ground) saw them trounce us 5—0. We were not in the same class, although we didn't play badly.

On the way back to our hotel that night, I couldn't help feeling sorry for the many Sunderland supporters who had made the long journey to Tottenham, with their confidence in us boosted by the great 1—1 draw we had earned at Roker on the previous Saturday.

When we had equalised, hundreds of our loyal fans had spilled on to the pitch to thump our backs. They really believed that we had it in us to beat the Spurs at the second meeting.

But they were disappointed—and so was I, for I realised then how difficult it is to get to Wembley, and brooded on the luck of the draw which had paired us with the Spurs and not with, say, Barnsley or Sheffield United, whom I am sure we could have beaten.

Little did I think then that I would be back at Tottenham in a week — to play for the England Under-23 team against West Germany.

I was completely surprised by my selection, I had no idea that I was even being considered. But it came as grand consolation after my Cup disappointment.

Although Sunderland have been my only professional club, I was born in Liverpool, grew up as a Liverpool supporter, and was at Anfield for three years as an amateur.

In 1954, I was a member of the Liverpool Boys' team which won the English Schools Trophy. I had as a team-mate, Derek Temple, who is now with Everton.

I wanted to become a Liverpool first-team player, and when I played for England in a series of Youth internationals, my hopes were that Liverpool would offer me professional terms.

But they didn't, so when George Curtis — now our chief coach at Roker Park, and then manager of the England Youth team—invited me to meet Alan Brown, the Sunderland manager, in December, 1957, I accepted his offer to turn professional.

At first, I was a part-timer. I held a printing union card as an apprentice and it was only as recently as last February, that I became a full-time professional for Sunderland.

After playing in 12 reserve games I was promoted to Sunderland's League side in rather unusual circumstances.

In September, 1958, Sunderland were bottom of the Second Division and there was a big shuffle for a game with Ipswich. In fact, 22 players were ordered to report to the ground before the game and Mr. Brown then picked eleven. I was at left-back and Jimmy McNab and Cecil Irwin also made their debut.

I have always been a natural, left-footed defender but since I have been under the coaching influence of George Curtis and manager Alan Brown, I have been able to develop power in my other foot, too. In addition to that memorable Cup clash with Spurs, the season 1960-61 produced lots of thrills for me.

One was when I helped to put my old club, Liverpool, out of the F.A. Cup, at Anfield, in the third round; then came a convincing win over Arsenal, at Roker, followed by a hard-fought-for victory at Norwich which really had our supporters sky-high with delight.

Big Charlie Hurley, our centre-half, got the only goal that day. Charlie was a key man in our greatly improved showing last season.

My 100th League game for Sunderland came, appropriately, in the big Wear-Tees "derby" meeting with Middlesbrough.

I don't regret moving to Sunderland. I have settled down very well in the north-east, have married a local girl and am looking forward to playing cricket again this summer—I was a batsman for Lancashire Schoolboys. Anyway, I hope to play for a club near Sunderland.

These things apart, my greatest hope is that I shall be at Sunderland when they win back their rightful place in the First Division. I believe it to be only a question of time.

We have a fine young team (average age 23) with just enough experience to make it "tick", and in Stan Anderson, we have one of the finest wing-halves and skippers in football.

I have not yet tasted First Division Soccer and I am anxious to gain that experience before long.

Sunderland are a First Division team by tradition. Our supporters expect us to get back, and if I know my colleagues at Roker, they will be striving might and main to achieve that goal next season.

Everybody goes for...

Men's Knitted Casual Shirts— illustrated 41/6. Also Swimwear, Leisure Slacks and Shorts for life in the wide open spaces. For nearest stockist write to

DOUGLAS WARNE & CO. LTD.,
14-15 Charterhouse Buildings, Goswell Road, London, E.C.I.

MY TARGET IS UNCLE FRED'S RECORD

says IAN LAWTHER
Sunderland and Northern Ireland

UNCLE FRED started it all. The family Soccer tradition was begun in the late 1920's and early 1930's by my uncle, Fred Roberts, the former Northern Ireland and Glentoran centre-forward.

Now I am trying to emulate Uncle Fred, who holds the Irish League goal-scoring record of 90 goals in one season. But I have a long way to go. I netted 17 times last season, my first in League Soccer, and had passed that total by the half-way stage this season.

My elder brother, Derek, also carries on the family tradition. He is centre-half with Irish League club Coleraine.

I, too, was a centre-half at one time. In fact, I started as a schoolboy player in that position. After school I joined the well-known Boyland Boys' Club

CHARLEY HURLEY . . . "one of the best centre-halves I have seen," says Lawther.

team in Belfast and it was then that I switched to the forward line.

But it wasn't until a long time afterwards that I became a centre-forward. My favourite position was either at inside or outside-right.

I am one of the few lads who turned down a chance to join Manchester United. As a 15-year-old I had a six-week trial at Old Trafford, but I didn't fancy the set-up at all. Perhaps it was because I was young and rather home-sick.

So I returned to Belfast and played as an amateur with Crusaders and the amateur League club, East Belfast. While I was playing for East Belfast I won my first representative honour—an Irish international youth cap.

After a period as Crusaders' first team centre-forward, in the Irish League, I was approached by Sunderland's Northern Ireland scout, Tom Coulter, and manager Alan Brown.

Mr. Brown had made an unsuccessful trip to Belfast in a bid to sign John Crossan, but I agreed to go to Roker Park for a trial. After five weeks there Mr. Brown said he wanted me to sign professional forms for Sunderland.

But first, I had to go through the formality of signing professional forms for Crusaders. Then I was transferred to Sunderland.

So I came to Roker Park, and to a depressing atmosphere, for Sunderland had been relegated for the first time in their proud history, and many famous stars like Len Shackleton, Ray Daniel,

Billy Bingham and Charlie Fleming, had moved on.

After only six months in Sunderland's reserve team I was flung into the Second Division side. That was at the start of the 1959-60 season.

It was the beginning of a very worrying time for me. The Roker Park fans were impatient with the club's efforts to fight back to the First Division. As the centre-forward, I was one of the most criticised players in the team.

Nobody seemed to appreciate that I was only 20, in my first season of League Soccer, and in a side that was painstakingly being re-built from youth team level by Mr. Brown.

But our manager always encouraged me most when things seemed blackest and my end of the season tally of 17 goals wasn't too bad.

I won my first cap for Ireland in April, 1960, when I was picked to play against Wales at Wrexham. Unfortunately we lost 2—3 and I didn't score.

But I am sure better times are ahead for Sunderland—and myself. At Roker Park we now have some of the finest players in the country. Charlie Hurley is a really brilliant ball-player and one of the best centre-halves I have ever seen.

Our captain, Stan Anderson, is another great player, and when one realises that our team is made up of players in their early 20's, then promotion in the next season or so seems a certainty.

What a fabulous day that will be when Sunderland get back to the First Division! They are a great club and deserve to be on top.

As for myself, I am hoping that my game will improve under the first-class coaching of manager Brown and coach George Curtis. At 21, I have plenty of time to look forward to more international caps with Ireland.

Even after only one international appearance I can understand why Ireland do so well. Peter Doherty has inspired young players to pull out their best and, what is more important, he lets them play their own game.

But somehow I don't think I will ever equal my Uncle Fred's record—90 goals in a season is quite a formidable task!

THE YOUNG ONES . . .

DEREK FORSTER . . . age 15 . . . occupation, goalkeeper . . . Sunderland's and the Football League's youngest player. Here he is against Leicester at the start of this season. And, on the right—another teenage top of the pops.

WHAT A SHOCK FOR CELTIC !

They sent for me, then discovered I was only 14

by JIMMY McNAB, Sunderland

NO youngster could have had a better footballing background than I, and no one could be more proud of carrying a famous Sunderland name like McNab into action at Roker.

One of my predecessors in Sunderland's pre-war half-back line was Alex McNab. He was left-half in Sunderland's F.A. Cup-winning team of 1937.

Like me, Alex McNab was a Scot. He was born in Glasgow, and I was born in Denny, near Stirling, famous as the home of Billy Steel, the great little Scottish international inside-forward. I was keen on football from my earliest days, for my uncle Bert played as a full-back with Dunipace and Petershill. He also holds the record number of Scottish junior caps—16.

With this football atmosphere, it was, I suppose, natural that I should do well at the game at school. I began as a wing-half and, in 1954-55, was capped for the Scottish Boys against Wales and England.

At about that time, when I was 14, I was offered a trial by Celtic, but it was a mistake! The Celts manager, Mr. Jimmy McGrory, had thought I was 16 when he sent for me.

When he found out just how young I was, he sent me home, telling me that I would hear from the club in due course. But I didn't, and nor did anything come

McNAB

||||||||||||||||||||||||||||||||||

of another trial I had a little later, as a left-winger with Partick Thistle.

While I was playing for the Stirlingshire County side I was spotted by a Sunderland scout. Two years later, they contacted me with a firm offer to go to Roker.

In the meantime, I had been playing as a juvenile with Denny Rovers, and was working as an agricultural fitter's apprentice.

I had no intention of leaving Scotland when Sunderland came for me again, but my father persuaded me to try my luck in English football.

Mr. Bill Murray was the Sunderland manager in those days, and he was very kind. He saw to it that I got plenty of coaching and advice, and also found me a part-time job as a motor mechanic.

The Sunderland "giants" then were Len Shackleton, Ray Daniel, Billy Elliott, Trevor Ford and Co., but I hardly ever saw them, let alone play alongside them. I was just a humble junior on the staff and, of course, my part-time job kept me away from the ground for long periods.

One of my greatest mentors at Roker was coach Arthur Wright who in his day, was a fine wing-half and has been for more than 25 years with the club. He taught me the arts of half-back play,

and later on George Curtis arrived to reinforce the Sunderland coaching staff, under manager Alan Brown.

In September, 1958, I made my League debut in unusual circumstances. Before the home game with Ipswich Town, 22 players were ordered to report to the dressing room. The seniors had been having a rough time and everyone knew that there was to be a "shake-up". I was one of the younger players told to report, and half-an-hour before the kick-off manager Brown picked the team to meet Ipswich. I was in at left-half, in front of Len Ashurst, who was also making his debut.

After ten successive League games I

" I don't know why you are so tired. You say you scored today so you can't have been running about ! "

broke my right ankle and was out of action for three months. When I recovered, Reg Pearce was holding down my place and the team was beginning to play really well.

Then Reg broke a leg, I won back my place, and have been a regular for two seasons. However, another disappointment was in store for me. Just before Sunderland's F.A. Cup sixth round replay at Tottenham I went down with influenza.

I will always remember our tie with Spurs, at Roker, when Willie McPheat scored our equaliser in the 1—1 draw and our fans invaded the pitch; and our grand win over Arsenal, in the fourth round, also at Roker. Stan Anderson, who was a most inspiring skipper and right-half, scored both our goals that day.

There has been a great revival in Sunderland's fortunes in the past twelve months. We have a fine, young side and some of our football has been a wonderful tonic for our supporters, who are flocking back.

I have changed my style completely since I became a Sunderland player. As a wing-half, I used to hold the ball far too long. It was Arthur Wright who taught me the error of my ways and converted me into the defensive half-back that I am now.

This is essential to the strategic plans of Sunderland's half-back line for Stan Anderson is primarily an attacking player who likes to go up in close support of his forwards.

SUNDERLAND:

Back row—Smith, Irwin, Kiernan, Ashurst, O'Neill, Lewis, Richardson. Second row—Hurley, Overfield, Hooper, Wakeham, Harvey, Hird, McPheat, J. Watters (physiotherapist), Jones (training staff). Third row—Anderson, Herd, McNab, Mr. S. Collins (chairman), Mr. A. Brown (manager), Clough, Fogarty, Lawther. Front row—Usher, Sharkey, Dillon, Murray, Stiff, Montgomery, Potter.

LEN ASHURST
Sunderland

LAUGH A MINUTE

(But always we

Stan Anderson (left), captain of England, exchanges pennants with the French captain before the start of an Under-23 match at Bristol.

by

STAN ANDERSON

Sunderland

SINCE I was a small boy playing about the nearby pit village of Horden, Co. Durham, I always wanted to play for Sunderland. Now, after eight years as a first-team player, Sunderland are still the only club for me. They are my local team and, I hope, always will be!

Many people in Soccer say it is better for a player to get away from his home-town club. But I have no complaints about the way I have been treated at Roker Park although the fortunes of Sunderland have gone up and down.

I am only 26, so I have been lucky to pack in a lot of experience since I made my League debut with Sunderland—then in the First Division—at the age of 18.

The most enjoyable part of my career at Roker Park was in the days of Len Shackleton, Ray Daniel, Bill

Fraser, Ken Chisholm and the "old gang". It was a laugh a minute in those days with that crowd of personalities and, although I was the odd-man out in that team of stars, they were all my pals.

I played for the East Durham Schoolboy representative side and in 1949 won three England schoolboy international caps.

Dennis Viollet and Jeff Whitefoot were my colleagues in those schoolboy international games, and Johnny Haynes was a reserve.

I signed for Sunderland immediately after leaving school and also started training as a plumber. When I was 17 I signed full-time professional forms and a year later made my first-team debut, at Roker Park, against Portsmouth.

Oddly enough, I played my last First Division game against Portsmouth, too. While we were at Fratton Park we heard that Sunderland had been relegated to the Second Division.

I have made seven appearances for England's Under-23 international side, played in two England "B" internationals and was first reserve for the full England side in Denmark six years ago.

Looking back to our old side at Sunderland, when "Shack" and Co. were the stars, I don't agree with the people who say it wasn't a successful team. We finished fourth and sixth in the First Division with that side and appeared in two F.A. Cup semi-finals.

Ray Daniel, a great ball-player, loved to develop new tricks which Len Shackleton tried to outdo. Ray always took it rather seriously when his leg was pulled in the dressing rooms.

WITH THE OLD GANG

had the boxing gloves ready)

For weeks Ray, a Welsh international centre-half, practised a trick with a half-a-crown. He would spin the coin and catch it neatly on the end of his toe. When Ray first did this trick in the dressing room we were all astounded and I remember him saying to Shackleton: "How about that Len?"

We heard nothing more about Ray's amazing trick for a couple of days. Then "Shack" came into the dressing room one morning before training and said: "Ray, you know that trick you did with the half-a-crown the other day. Was this what you meant?"

To Ray's amazement, he pulled out a silver coin spun it in the air caught it on the end of his toe and with a deft flick sent it flying into his breast pocket!

Ray Daniel never tried that trick again when Len Shackleton was around! Cliff Jones of Tottenham Hotspur, has several variations of this trick now. I understand he can flick the coin on to his head, toe, thigh and into his pocket.

There was always a set of boxing gloves handy at Roker Park. Any dressing room difference was settled with the boxing gloves in the gymnasium. Boxing promoter Jack Solomons would have been very interested in some of the hectic battles in the gym—but afterwards the two battered and bruised combatants would be the best of pals!

I still chuckle at some of the wisecracks that used to be bandied around. One incident I recall was when we were due to play a match on the New York Dodgers' baseball ground during our tour of the United States.

We were lined up before the game while the loud-speaker announcer introduced us by name and quoted our transfer fee value . . . "Ray Daniel, centre-half-back, 90,000 dollars; Len Shackleton, inside-forward, 60,000 dollars," etc., etc.

"I wonder what they are going to say for you?" cracked Ray Daniel, nudging me as he beamed at his own 90,000 dollar tag. Of course, as a local player, I hadn't cost a transfer fee at all and I was hoping they wouldn't call out: "Stan Anderson, right-half-back, 30 dollars," which, of course, was the American equivalent of the £10 signing on fee I got from Sunderland.

It is a fact that Ray knew his transfer value in dollars, roubles, pesetas, and lire.

I remember another crack from those days. I won't mention the two players concerned, but you might be able to guess. We had had a bad game that day and one of my team-mates turned towards another player in the dressing room and asked in a confidential whisper: "Where is it?"

"Where's what, pal?" replied the other player.

"The blinking hole in the pitch where you've been hiding for 90 minutes," came the snappy answer.

Our goalkeeper, Willie Fraser, was a grand type. I remember his first game for us—it was against Tottenham and it was the best display of goalkeeping I have ever seen. I remember Fraser's most embarrassing moment, too. He was still on National Service and we were playing Portsmouth at Fratton Park.

Little did Field-Marshal Montgomery know, when he shook hands with Sunderland's goalkeeper in a pre-match presentation to the team, that he was shaking hands with a National Service private who was absent without leave and who had to face several days' "jankers" when he got back to his unit the next day!

As a wing-half I agree with Danny Blanchflower's theories about wing-half-play. Danny says: "I am not worried what the inside-forward does. My aim is to make the inside-forward worry about what I am doing as a wing-half."

I have my critics who accuse me of being too much of an attacking wing-half, but I make no apologies for that.

In my opinion there are too many managers in football who adopt the negative attitude to the game. The trouble is that when they are players, they agree that good football is the only way, yet as soon as they become manager they adopt the dreadfully dull "safety first" attitude.

Too many teams try to hold on to a draw when they are playing away from home. If they are good enough to draw then surely it is better to think positively that they are good enough to win.

That is one of the reasons why the crack Continental sides are so much better. I noticed it when I saw Barcelona play against Newcastle United.

Barcelona were three goals down in the first-half yet they still played their normal slick-passing game. Even when they reduced the arrears to 3—2 they still kept to their calm, deliberate style and were rewarded by a 4—3 win.

ACTION!

This high-flying raid by Ambrose Fogarty, of Sunderland, caused no damage. But it did make Joe Turner, Scunthorpe goalkeeper, leap to panic stations.

OUR FUTURE IS BRIGHT WITH THE YOUNG ONES

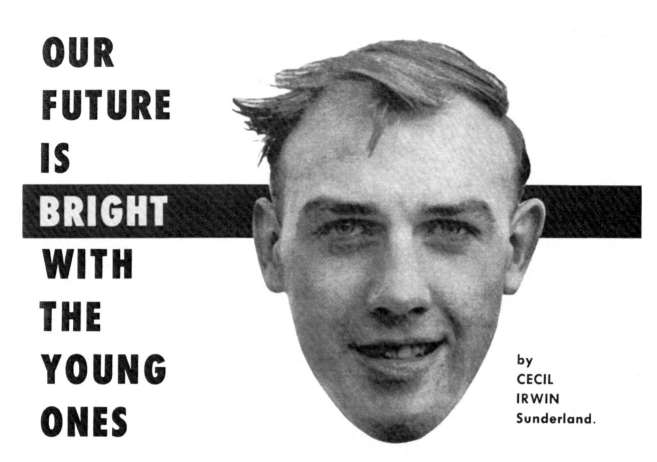

by
**CECIL
IRWIN
Sunderland.**

ON the day that Alan Brown quit Burnley to become manager of Sunderland, I left the North East for an unsuccessful trial at Turf Moor. We probably passed each other on the way!

A month later, I was back in the North East. By Christmas, 1957, I had signed amateur forms for Sunderland. I was then 15. Now I have established a first-team place at Roker. But I am only one of several youngsters who have given the Sunderland team a complete "facelift" in the past twelve months.

Look at our side in February, 1962. For the game against our strongest promotion challengers, Leyton Orient, we fielded seven teenagers. Injuries and temporary loss of form by some of our recognised first-team men had something to do with that, of course.

But the inclusion of young lads like Jimmy Davison, Jim Montgomery, Dickie Rooks and Willie McPheat, for instance, proved that Sunderland's youth policy was at last beginning to break through.

When our manager is confident enough in his youngsters to be able to leave out experienced performers like Brian Clough and Colin Nelson, then we, in turn, feel bound to do our darndest to justify Mr. Brown's faith.

Sunderland are determined to regain their First Division place and I feel sure that our turn is only just around the corner. For the North East to be without a First Division side is unthinkable!

Pardon me for sounding so pro-Sunderland, but I was a fervent fan of theirs. I was born and brought up in Ashington—which produced the Milburn and Charlton brothers—none of whom played for Sunderland—and my ambition was to play for the Roker Park club one day.

I was a centre-half in my schooldays. I played for East Northumberland boys in the English Schools Trophy and also for the Northumberland County XI. It was during this period that I was converted from centre-half to full-back. I was a big lad for my age.

When I left school I went for 16 weeks' preliminary training with the National Coal Board for a job down the pit. That was in the summer of 1957. It was then that I had my invitation to go to Burnley for a month's trial. One of their North-Eastern scouts had seen me play schoolboy football.

Burnley have taken quite a few of their first-team players from my part of the North East, so I wasn't all that surprised when their offer came.

But I didn't settle at Turf Moor and returned to Ashington when my month was up. Then Sunderland's chief scout, Mr. Jack Hall, came for me and offered me a ground-staff job at Roker.

In my first season with Sunderland, I was a member of the junior team which won the Northern Intermediate League Cup. I also got into the England Youth side against Wales and went to Bulgaria for the international youth tournament there, playing against Rumania and Greece.

In the England side with me were Nobby Stiles, of Manchester United, Geoff Hurst, of West Ham, Malcolm Beard, of Birmingham City and Dave Bacuzzi, of Arsenal. All have played in First Division Soccer regularly since then. I hope I'm not too long in catching them up.

My Sunderland League début came when we were going through a lean spell and Mr. Brown decided to make several changes. Against Ipswich Town, Len Ashurst, Jimmy McNab and I were all "blooded" together. But we lost 1—2.

That was the only senior game I had that season. I wasn't really ready for Second Division football then. I began the following campaign in the reserves and had a few first-team matches—but only when first-choice Colin Nelson was hurt.

Not until the autumn of 1961 did I get my first chance to stake a claim for a regular League place.

I was brought in for the match against Scunthorpe in September, and have been in ever since then.

As a boy I used to watch Arthur Wright give some fine wing-half displays for Sunderland. As coach he helped me enormously. So has Jackie Jones. And I mustn't forget George Curtis.

George is now manager of Brighton, but as coach he gave me invaluable tips when I was a "greenhorn" at Roker.

Two or three games in season 1961-62 stand out for me. There was our match against Walsall when Stan Anderson was hurt and we won 2—0, with ten men. And then the F.A. Cup clash with Southampton. A Roker crowd of 58,000 saw us win that thriller by 2—0.

When not playing or talking Soccer I enjoy sea fishing. It is a popular sport on the North East coast and I spend a lot of time at it. I also play cricket.

BRIAN CLOUGH
Sunderland and England

STAN ANDERSON
Sunderland and England

GOAL DIFFERENCE SHOULD BE USED TO DECIDE PROMOTION

So Says...
CHARLIE HURLEY
of Sunderland and Eire

I owe Sunderland something and I mean to repay my debt this season, because it has been hanging over my head too long.

I was one of the Sunderland team relegated for the first time in the history of the club five years ago. I know I wasn't responsible, but I was a member of the team that went down and that makes it my duty to get them back where they rightfully belong.

Mind you, we should have had one more chance of getting back last season than we did have.

Chelsea pipped us for second place in the Second Division and promotion, by .401 of a goal.

Who ever heard of .401 of a goal?

This goal average deciding issues as important as promotion and relegation is utter nonsense. When teams finish level on points there should be a play-off on a neutral ground.

Maybe I have a bee in my bonnet about goal average, after all, we didn't only fail to get

promotion because of a fraction of a goal, we were also relegated the same way.

I don't like mentioning the word, but if we have a jinx at Sunderland, then we were jinxed.

We're off now on another season, another chance of getting back to the First Division where we belong. But y'know, whatever happens in the future, I'll never forget one thing from the past. That game against Chelsea at Roker Park on the last Saturday of last season.

We hadn't even got to win it. We'd only to draw to go up.

It was a tremendous occasion, but I didn't even have one solitary butterfly beforehand. We were, I reckoned, stonewall certs.

In my nine years as a professional footballer I've never been in the really big-time, but I've had fairly big moments. Disappointments too, but nothing even one hundreth as bad as when we went off that field having lost 1-0.

I was shocked and shattered. I couldn't look up. If I had I'd have seen the faces of those wonderful fans of ours, if I was feeling bad, how must they have been feeling.

Near the end I asked the referee, "How long to go?"

He said, "Two minutes."

I came back with, "Can't you stretch it to five?"

I've never said that to a referee before and I've also never said to anyone I've ever played against what I said to the Chelsea centre-half Frank Upton, when he fouled me near the end. It wouldn't have happened either, hadn't I suddenly realised all our dreams, all our hopes, had gone for another year, that we weren't going to make it.

You'll notice I keep harping on about Sunderland deserving to be in the First Division, these aren't just words to me, I really mean what I say.

This is a wonderful club with a great bunch of players and a manager and staff who are with you all the way. I'll bet there aren't half a dozen clubs in the game which compare.

Yet the amazing thing, looking back over six years, is that I wasn't at all settled when I first came here. Manager Alan Brown had to talk practically the whole day before he could persuade me to leave Millwall and come to Roker Park.

I was born in Eire, but lived there only seven months. I'd been brought up in the South, I was happy with Millwall. I didn't see what the heck I could gain from moving North even though Sunderland was a big club.

There was no overnight change either, for the first couple of seasons I didn't really settle.

Then I found that the atmosphere of the club seeped into me, that these football crazy people around here were great folk, that Charlie

HOULDN'T DECIDE TION !

Hurley was being a bit daft lugging around a chip on his shoulder.

And am I glad that happened?

Now it's flat out for the First Division. Up there a player faces a lot of challenges.

Though winning promotion is the No. 1 target of the moment, my greatest ambition is to play in the F.A. Cup Final at Wembley and better still, to win a Cup medal.

After all, when you think of the thousands upon thousands of boys and men who play football, only a handful can ever point to an F.A. Cup medal and say: "I won that."

Then, in the First Division, you are among the best in the land, as a team you really find out how good you are.

As a player, in my case a centre-half, you really find out if you can cope with the best centre-forwards in the home countries.

My taste of the big stuff has more or less been confined to playing for Eire and against som First Division clubs in the Cup.

It has whetted my appetite for more. I am out to nail that jinx,

I went to a dance to find a girl friend—

—but my dancing didn't make girls 'friendly'!

—till a pal told me the secret of Escort's Sure Step System

Now I'm no longer lonely—

—the girls know my steps are sure !

Can't afford private lessons? Learn ball-room dancing at home! Send for exciting booklet 'Dance Escort'—FREE to readers of "Football Monthly"—which explains the miraculous SURE STEP system. Just send name and address to:

ESCORT DANCE INSTRUCTORS
Studio C.B.19. Harrogate
(or Rock 'n' Roll Course – send 4/6 P.O.)

CHARLIE HURLEY

Ten players in search of the ball . . . five photographers in search of a picture—and another one, on the other side, got this! Scene: the Northampton goalmouth during the rush hour in their victorious match with proud Sunderland.

Sunderland v. Southampton in a promotion battle. Nick Sharkey, Sunderland's centre-forward and a Scottish Under-23 international, seems to be floating on air as he rises with burly Cliff Huxford in a heading duel

In the shadow of Sunderland
legend Stan Anderson

BUT NOW I AM IN THE
TEAM ON MERIT
BY
MARTIN HARVEY
Sunderland

Ten days, that's all it took to change my entire soccer life. The ten days October 2nd to October 12th 1963.

On that first date I played for Sunderland against Plymouth. It wasn't my first game for the first team, but it was the start of my first real run it.

Up to then I'd been in the shadow of then Sunderland skipper and England internationalist Stan Anderson.

But in I went and in between then and the end of our promotion-winning season, I played 39 games on the trot. And seven games after I got in, Stan was transferred to Newcastle United.

Then, October 12th, I played for Ireland against Scotland in my home town of Belfast. In the process there disappeared another shadow that had been across my path. I had actually been preferred to Danny Blanchflower for the first time.

I'll tell you this, by the time Christmas came around I reckoned I didn't deserve anything. The old boy with the beard had moved in early on Martin Harvey.

I've heard it said I got the needle at having to stand behind Stan Anderson for the couple of seasons before I made the right half spot.

Not true, though I once got a bit huffy. It was the day we played against Bury and Brian Clough got the knee injury which finished his career. I was in for that game and thought that I did alright, but I was out again for the return next day.

So I said my piece to manager Alan Brown, then he said his, and I went down the stairs a whole lot happier than I'd climbed them. There was nothing dramatic about what Mr Brown said. Just that when I warranted a real step up, I would get it. I believed him and have never regretted it.

I suppose you must say I was 'soaked in the atmosphere' of the game as a nipper. For I was born in the same district of Belfast as Danny Blanchflower, Billy Bingham and Ian Lawther, who was a club-mate at Roker Park for several years.

Danny, Billy and Jimmy McIlroy used to play for a local team down the road. The wee fellow who used to give them the old 'come on' from

the touchline was myself.

And I'll tell you this, I'm glad now I'm something like 15 years younger than Danny. If I'd been a contemporary, I could still have been waiting for my first full cap, because, for my money, Danny was tops as a wing-half.

My first taste of organised football came with the Strand town (Belfast) primary school team. I was ten when I moved on to Ashfield Intermediate School.

A lad I called Dennis Hayes and myself were the first two from the school ever to win Irish schoolboy caps. We had such a good team we were chosen to a man to represent County Down in the Irish Schools' Cup. We beat County Antrim 11-1 in the final.

As a wing-half, 5'3" tall and weighing just 8st 6lb, I went for a trial with Burnley. At that time Mr Alan Brown had just left there to take over at Sunderland. Now of course, he has moved on to Sheffield Wednesday.

The first game I played in, I had signed for a trial only, my claret and amber jersey drooped six inches below my fingertips, my stocking tops had to be rolled over four times to make them look even presentable, my pants were hitched four times round my waistband. Despite all this, I reckoned I didn't do too badly.

I was told to come back a year later, but when Sunderland stepped in to offer me a job on the ground staff, I accepted.

Sunderland had five teams. Silksworth was the fifth. I was their outside-left in the early days and when you consider No. 11 is the last place on the team sheet, I was 55th from the first team keeper, reading downwards out of 55 players at Roker Park.

Outside-left Martin Harvey and I was played there until I added a bit of weight and height. Eventually I put on the inches and the pounds, now I am 5ft 11" and 12 st. and made my own position of right-half against Workington in a reserve fixture a couple of years after joining Sunderland.

My first-team debut came four years ago, against Plymouth Argyle. We drew 0-0, I thought I did fairly well, but I still had another two and a bit seasons of grooming ahead.

Now I realise everything was planned down to the last detail and that I was brought on in

exactly the right way for any young footballer. I'm not being big-headed but, even though my real experience consists of two-thirds of a season as a first team regular, plus about a dozen Irish caps, I feel a mature player because of what went before.

At the moment we're a step up on last season. In the First Division, it's where we should be. The whole club has a First Division air.

I hope we do well, I hope I do well, in an Irish jersey too. Both Ireland and Sunderland have young teams and I reckon both will thrive.

It's really great playing in the national team. A lot of that maturity I talked about earlier came from facing top player's like Italy's Sivori. I came across him in my first full international, I belted into a tackle early on and turfed him. He looked as if he was going to get up and have a go, so I got ready, but he changed his mind. Instead he made a right monkey of me a bit later on.

We were going for a ball running towards the Ireland goal, inches out in front, he flicked it back through my legs. I was left charging in on our own keeper! Sivori meanwhile was standing cheeky as you like with the ball at his feet.

Some time later I watched him on TV playing for Italy against Spain and he was laying about a Spanish defender like a heavy-weight champion. I reckon now if he had got up after that first tackle of mine, my career as an international might have been very short!

Mind you, though I class Sivori the greatest inside-forward I've faced up to so far, just a fraction ahead of Denis Law, I never worry who I am playing against, I treat every inside-forward as a great player, never mind whether he is a big name or an unknown.. That way, you're less liable to have a bad game.

I try to guard further against that by paying attention to superstition. As soon as I step into the main door of the ground we are playing on, I whip off my ring and watch. I just think it's lucky.

JIM MONTGOMERY
Sunderland

CHARLIE HURLEY
Sunderland

JOHNNY CROSSAN
Sunderland

CECIL IRWIN
Sunderland

The start of one of the most intense Cup battles ever known. A fierce Manchester United attack on the Sunderland goal in the first of their three Sixth Round meetings. Left to right: George Herd, Billy Foulkes, Cecil Irwin, Charlie Hurley, Maurice Setters, Jim Montgomery.

Snapped against a massed, roaring background of Roker Park fans, Charlie Hurley (No. 5, striped shirt), heads past Gordon West, Denis Stevens and Brian Labone, to start a goal-scoring movement which put Everton out of the Cup.

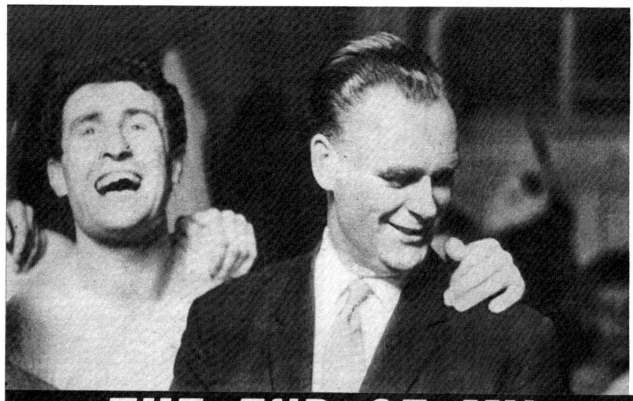

THE END OF MY SEVEN-YEAR ITCH!

by CHARLIE HURLEY

Sunderland and Eire

Sunderland are back in the First Division after six seasons of being in what was to them the wilderness of the Second. For Sunderland went down in 1958, in Hurley's first season with them.
Until then they had been the only First Division club never relegated and they have fought hard to get back.
Hurley, the only survivor of that relegated team, is in the picture (above) with manager Alan Brown.

THE pressure has been off now for a restful month. I feel as fresh as if I had come from a Turkish bath. The First Division lies ahead—for Sunderland are back in their rightful surroundings, having served six years in the Second Division.

If those last words read like a prison sentence then that is just how it has seemed to me. I was there—I'm the only playing survivor—when Second Division football was prescribed for the first time in Sunderland's history.

It has never seemed "right" for Sunderland to be in the Second, and our supporters have never accepted it.

Like men who have seen their birthright filched they backed the team passionately and impatiently during those six long seasons. Neither they nor I believe in second best.

If you feel that way then the road back can be long and hard, and disappointing.

In the two seasons before the last one I had two experiences I would not wish on anybody . . . we got the First Division door open, only to have it slammed on our fingers right at the end.

It was a wretched, numbing experience, and it went very deep in me because I felt so much about the team and game.

I can't have been the most pleasant person tó know or live with in the past two years when the tension took toll of my nerves. But at about this time last month, things changed.

Promotion was at last a reality and not the mocking mirage we had stalked the two previous seasons.

The pressure was even more intense last season because of those three tremendous Cup battles we had with Manchester United. Those games could easily have taken the edge off our League challenge.

I was made captain when Stan Anderson moved across the way to Newcastle. That appointment made me even more determined that we should win. And, of course, the job made me even more edgy.

I seem to have been waiting for something to happen, good or bad, at the end of each of my seven seasons at Roker Park.

In my first season it was the big drop.

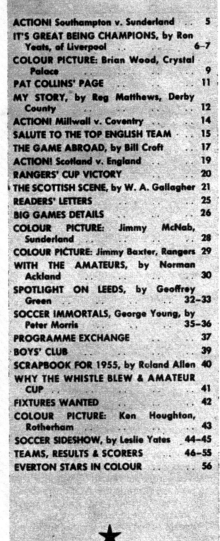

Charles Buchan's

FOOTBALL MONTHLY

June, 1964   **No. 154**

(Founded in 1951 by Charles Buchan, captain of Sunderland, Arsenal and England)

Edited by
JOHN THOMPSON
and **JOE SARL**

Assistant Editors:
PAT COLLINS
and **MALCOLM CUMMING**

CONTENTS

★

Moment of triumph! Hurley chaired by team-mate Jimmy McNab. The others: Cecil Irwin, Len Ashurst and Jimmy Montgomery.

What a miserable start that was to a young centre-half eager to go places! I was the first signing by manager Alan Brown—for £20,000, I read. I had gained two caps for Eire and had moved from Millwall in the Third Division to the First Division.

All set for fame .. !

My start with Sunderland should have prepared me for the heart-breaks and head-aches to come. The first two games were away. We lost 0—7 to Blackpool, then 0—6 to Burnley!

The Roker faithful, looking at me, the newcomer, must have wondered if their manager had bought a colander instead of a centre-half.

That season, my first, heralded Sunderland's first in the Second Division. The drop came at Portsmouth—a club who seem to have got mixed up with our fortunes a few times at most important moments.

On the last day of that fateful 1957-8 season it seemed that Pompey would be saved by goal average, no matter what we did to them. The same went for Newcastle, our neighbours. So it rested between our-selves and Leicester as to who should accompany the already doomed Sheffield Wednesday.

We pulled out all the stops at Ports-mouth and won 2—0. Then we had to wait for Leicester's result at Birmingham. Our kick-off had been 15 minutes earlier than theirs, so we sat in the bath and awaited our fate.

Leicester won 1—0 ... and down we went.

Like other clubs we were to find that it is hard to get off the slide once you get on it. In the next season we were for some time in danger of being relegated to the Third. In fact, it took us three more seasons to shape a side ready to bid for the return trip to the First.

So we come to the last day of the 1961-2 season. Liverpool were home and dry and Leyton Orient and ourselves were striving to go up with them. Orient were at home to Bury, we were at Swansea.

We had the same number of points, so the final reckoning could have been in decimals. Again our game had the earlier kick-off ...

and it was broadcast. So the Orient were in the nice, cosy position of being able to hear just what was required of them.

I was told there were dozens of transistors buzzing away as the fans at Leyton listened to our match. We grabbed the lead but were forced to a draw ... then sat and waited in the dressing room.

We heard we had been pipped—Orient won 2—0.

So to THE NEXT season—and again no come-back. If we had beaten Chelsea, even taken a point off them, we would have gone up.

We could, and should, have done that in our last home game, but little Tommy Harmer de-flected one home and we were left, unable to do anything but wait until Chelsea met Portsmouth (here they are again) at Stamford Bridge the fol-lowing Tuesday. They won right enough—7—0.

I remember feeling that we really couldn't ex-pect Pompey to do our job for us, yet I kept hoping until flashes began to come in telling of Chelsea sailing onwards and upwards.

So to last season and April 11 at The Dell. We had drawn a goalless game with the Saints. We awaited the Preston-Portsmouth (again!) result.

Our manager, Alan Brown, and some directors were in the Southampton board room, listening to the results. There was bedlam in our dressing room when we heard that North End had drawn (good old Pompey!) and we were up.

Sitting in that Southampton dressing-room and savouring that long-awaited moment made up for everything. I was glad for Alan Brown. He has had to put up with so much; he had needed the patience of Job as he planned for such a moment.

He had done it as thoroughly and as efficiently as anything else he does.

We had a common bond right then, the feeling that we had been in it together from the beginning. Of course, he has since continually pushed the praise over to the team.

But I take time here to pay him the tribute he deserves so much.

The team HAVE earned their place in the First Division. More than half of this Sunderland side have been brought up from the junior teams. ALL of them have backed me right up to the hilt.

With the average age less than 24 I confess I sometimes feel very fatherly towards them. They have learned well, they will go on doing so, for with this youthfulness there is also a well-balanced experience ... and a ton of first-class football, because that is what we like to play.

It has been a long wait, but a worthwhile one. Now we can look our supporters right in the eyes again. And we will give them plenty to cheer next season.

That's my pledge, and that of my team.

CHARLIE HURLEY (front)
LEN ASHURST, CECIL
IRWIN, of Sunderland

SUNDERLAND

English Second Division Runners-Up 1963-64

Left to right—back row—Cecil Irwin, Martin Harvey, Jim Montgomery, Charlie Hurley, Jimmy McNab, Len Ashurst. Front—Brian Usher, George Herd, Nick Sharkey, Johnny Crossan, George Mulhall.

JIMMY McNAB
Sunderland

IT'S EASY TO STAND AND STARE

CHARLIE HURLEY . . . helped off, injured, watched by ex-manager Hardwick.

L AST season I improved my football education . . . by sitting in the stands. A groin injury kept me out of business for two months. I got closer to the fans, saw more of the game.

And you would be surprised at the things you learn when you're not playing!

One story was that I was finished . . . that I would never kick another ball. Even my grocer, who saw me often enough and had the gen from the horse's mouth, as it were, got worried.

Fans stopped me in the streets to ask if and when I would be back again. That's not unusual. In Sunderland, more than in any other place I know, the people reckon to be part of the club.

We have an intense and critical following. They will back you come hell and high-water . . . as they proved last season, even though we gave them little to cheer.

There are no better-behaved fans, and they are as jealous of our traditions as is the club and players. So, as I have said, they stopped me, and asked—when was I coming back?

Anyway, when I had to sit among the crowd, listening, I found that I was more tolerant than they about short-comings on the field. Perhaps that is understandable; I took the players' view. Yet, I had to be careful—for it is much easier to "play" the game from the stands! I am

not a good spectator; I don't go out of my way to watch games. Always I have the feeling that I should be out there playing, especially when the lads are having a tough time . . . as we were.

I learned again just what goals mean in this game. You can have all the theories you like about it, but the fellow who gets a foot or a head to the ball at the right moment —he's the darling of the Gods.

And there are no bad goals . . . every one is a good one!

All right, I envy the fellows who score goals. If I had to start in this game again I would want to be an inside-forward—any one of the three positions would do. Because I, too, love to get a goal.

I've got some even as a centre-half. And believe me there is no thrill to equal that of the goal-scorer.

Be honest. As a football fan ask yourself: How long do you remember the fact that one of your defenders kicked the ball off the line—even twice in a match? Then, how much longer do you relish the moment when one of your team scored?

I think of myself as an attacker and I want to have a dip at goal far more often than we are able to do these days. I'm a defender, but I often feel that today too many forwards want to walk the ball in.

Some players have the born knack of being on the spot. We had such a player in Brian Clough. He was one of the last of his breed. It is a tragedy that injury forced him out

CHARLIE HURLEY, of Sunderland, tells what it's like

BRIAN CLOUGH . . . one of the last of his breed.

HURLEY . . . after victory —jubilation.

of the game so early. Dominic Sharkey is another good player who loves to have a crack from anywhere. If he were six inches taller he'd be a world-beater.

Brian was goal-greedy. He could play quite a bit out of range, but he never felt he had done his job unless he was banging them in. I thought he sometimes had great games even when he failed to score. He didn't.

There were other times when, without doing anything really great, he would suddenly whip a couple home. That was a good match in his book . . . he had done his job.

I understand his feelings. On the rare times when I move up with the ball—unless I'm up for a corner or free-kick— I feel an urge to try my luck anywhere from around 35 yards. I'm always telling myself that one of these Saturday afternoons my aim will be right and one shot will go in.

Meantime, my job is to try and stop them going in at OUR end.

I never was so relieved to get back into things as I was last February when my long wait was over. As I have said, I learned quite a lot when sitting in the stand and watching the other fellows getting on with it.

One of them was that while you can see and hear more up aloft, there is nothing like being out there on the park with the lads.

Nothing at all . . . !

DOMINIC SHARKEY . . . he could be a world-beater.

to be a looker-on (injured) instead of a man of action

Star Strip—CHARLIE HURLEY

GEORGE HERD
Sunderland

by NEIL MARTIN

Sunderland

I'M still a young man, but when I look back I am amazed just how much has been crammed into my six years in the game at League level, in Scotland and in England.

I seem to have done it all. Scaled the heights of international Soccer (in the World Cup) and played for the Scottish League. And plumbed the depths of despair even to the point of signing on for the dole!

I first played inside-forward at Tranent Public School, Edinburgh (the 'Public' is just a name, it doesn't indicate a rich young man's seminary) and when I left at 15 I joined Tranent Arsenal, a Scottish Junior side.

While there I was spotted by Alloa, signed as a part-timer (I was serving an apprenticeship as a mining engineer), and stayed there for a season-and-a-half before transferring to Queen of the South.

It was while with Queens that the dole incident occurred. I had signed full-time for them and was the only full-timer on their books, when I was offered terms — as a part-timer again. *I refused to sign and drew my dole until Walter Galbraith took me to Hibernian.*

I remained with Hibs for two seasons and in 1964-65 was really among the goals, scoring 40 in something like 42 games.

It was probably because of my goal-

You name it, I've done it —even going on the dole!

scoring activities that Mr. Ian McColl chose me for the Scotland side in three of the World Cup qualifying games against Italy, Finland and Poland, but unfortunately we were pipped by Italy for a place in the memorable finals.

I was also chosen three times for the Scottish League side and strangely enough my first game for the League was at Roker Park against the English League when we were robbed of victory in the last minute to draw 2-2.

I had no idea then that I would one day be proudly wearing the Sunderland colours but at the beginning of last season (bearing in mind my previous goal tally, which included four goals in a game on three occasions), I felt that I would like to try my luck in England.

I asked for a transfer and was delighted when in October, 1965, Mr. McColl, my mentor in the international field, asked me to join him at Sunderland. It was the chance I had been seeking and I grabbed it.

Although I didn't set the scoreboard alight last season—I scored only 8 goals —at least I finished as joint top-scorer with George Mulhall.

You will gather that I did not find it quite as easy as I had thought to switch from Scottish to English Soccer. Goals were much harder to come by, not particularly from any weaknesses in our own team, but chiefly because of the stronger English defences.

They are much, much tighter than in Scotland and I am only too well aware that this new season is not going to be easy. With Hibs I was scoring goals even when playing on the wings, for when Jock Stein became manager he tried me on both left and right wings as well as at inside-forward.

At Roker I was switched to centre-forward for the last six games of last season, with Jim Baxter on my left, and I don't by any means envisage an easy passage against such famous pivots as Mike England, Jackie Charlton, Ron Yeats, Brian Labone, Vic Mobley, etc.

In fact, most English defences appear to play two centre-halves, and the twin-striker method seems to be the only way round it.

But we have one or two cards up our sleeves, and I still feel that we shall give a good account of ourselves, always provided that we get a few of the breaks in the early part of the season.

We have the players and the spirit and if I can hit form and get only half the goals I scored in my last season with Hibs we will give any English League team a run for their money.

Neil Martin misses as he slides to take the ball from Gordon Marshall, of Newcastle.

ALEX McLAUGHLAN
Sunderland

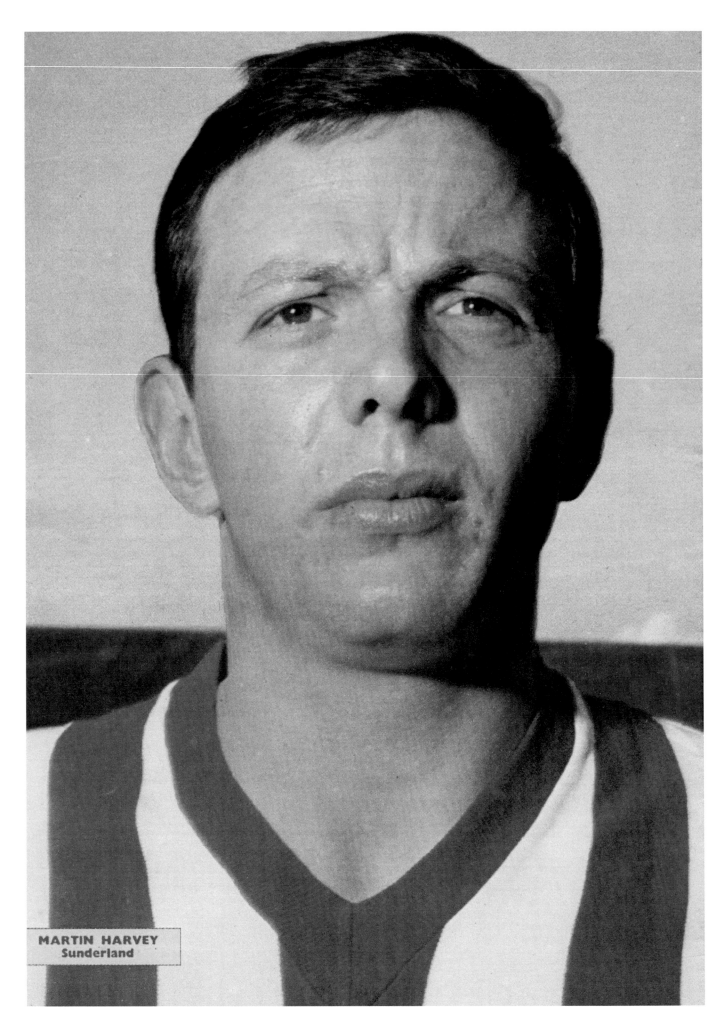

MARTIN HARVEY
Sunderland

UNFORGETTABLE!

... that was the scene when we went up

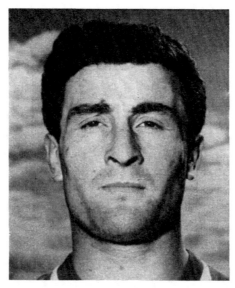

I AM not exactly a newcomer to the Soccer scene, and obviously, from my years in the game I have many memories — some happy, some perhaps a little sad.

But as is the case with many people in almost every walk of life, there is one moment that stands out. One unforgettable scene that will be indelibly printed on my mind no matter how long I live.

It happened as recently as 1964, the year when proud Sunderland, after a spell in the Second Division, returned to their natural habitat in the premier Division.

And it was fitting that the scene should be set at the club's famous ground at Roker Park.

The game was against Charlton Athletic and we needed two points to ensure promotion. The match was not particularly outstanding, apart from the tension, and the fact that our opponents were not giving anything away.

No, the flash-point was the sound of the final whistle.

That was it! We knew we had made it and so did 50,000 of our supporters, not one of whom had any wish to leave the ground. The din was terrific, we shook hands, slapped backs, and freely expressed the joy of our achievement.

But the crowd wanted more, and, in fact, the whole team had to run not one but *two* laps of honour before we could disappear into the dressing rooms and convince ourselves that we were in fact back "home"—in the First Division.

It was a great day for me personally because this was a team victory, an achievement after long months of struggle, of sweat and of strain. And the

by
CHARLIE HURLEY
Sunderland

fruits of final victory tasted sweeter than the finest vintage wine.

It wasn't (I hope) the culmination of my career—I hope to enjoy many more successes before I hang up my boots. But I was proud to have been a part of this successful team, particularly as it was achieved (for me) in a country I had adopted.

Not that I had any choice in that matter I was born in Cork City, Southern Ireland and my parents brought me to England at the ripe old age of seven months to set up home in Hornchurch, Essex.

It was there, at Sutton Secondary Boys School, that I first tasted competitive Soccer, playing several times for Essex Schoolboys, and having a trial for London Boys which got me nowhere.

Even in those far-off days, I was firmly settled as a centre-half and on leaving

school at 15, I took a job as an apprentice toolmaker and played for Rainham Youth Club.

Bill Voisey, of Millwall, saw me play on the losing side (0-1) in a Youth Cup Final and had a word with me, eventually persuading me to sign as an amateur.

I was not terribly excited about this as I had already had a trial with Arsenal, but at 15 I was way out of my class when playing with 18-year-olds.

I also had played for West Ham Juniors and they offered me a ground staff job. But the money wasn't sufficient to tempt me to give up my apprenticeship.

Imagine, therefore, my surprise when, on returning from a trip to Germany with an Essex Boys (Under-16½) team, I discovered that Millwall manager Charlie Hewitt had been to see my family, and persuaded them to agree to my signing full-time pro. at 17.

This, despite the fact that he had never seen me play!

I stayed at Millwall for four years and moved at 21 to my present berth in the North East. I have collected 30 International caps for Southern Ireland through the years—the first when I was still at Millwall and only 20.

I had actually been chosen for my country at 18, while I was in the army doing my National Service, but an injury prevented me from playing. I made my International debut at Dalymount Park in 1957 against England in a World Cup qualifying round.

Forgive my national pride when I say that we played a blinder, most people agreeing that we fully deserved to win. Had we done so it would have meant a play-off (against England) for a place in the last 16 in the 1958 series in Sweden. But we managed only a 1-1 draw and England went forward.

Other than our promotion game v. Charlton, I would rate our three Cup games v. Manchester United in 1963-64 as one of my outstanding experiences.

In the first game we were leading 1-0 when I scored an own goal, but we were leading 3-1 with only minutes to go when United levelled at three-all.

In the replay (after extra time) we ended level again at 2-2, but in the second replay (at Huddersfield) they trounced us 5-1. I often wondered what would have happened had I not "scored" that own goal in the first game!

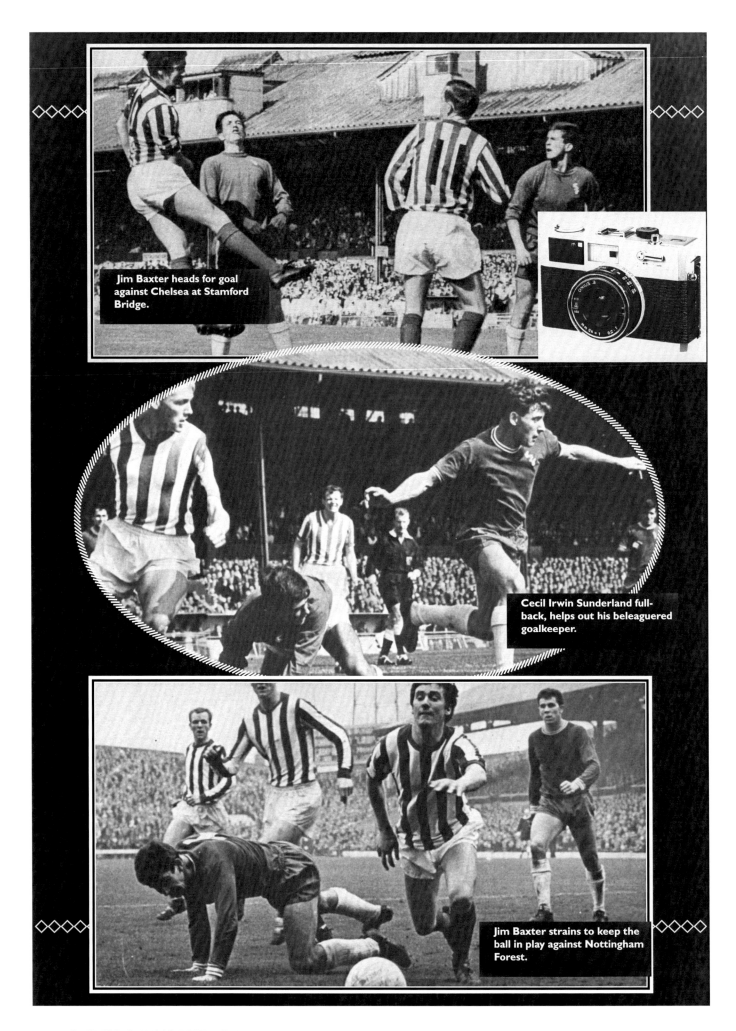

Jim Baxter heads for goal against Chelsea at Stamford Bridge.

Cecil Irwin Sunderland full-back, helps out his beleaguered goalkeeper.

Jim Baxter strains to keep the ball in play against Nottingham Forest.

JOHN PARKE
Sunderland

THE FIRST CUP FINAL IN MAY

MAY DAY 1937. In Moscow's Red Square the Russians were putting on their annual display of military might; at Swansea's St. Helen's Ground Dai Davies and Arnold Dyson were scoring centuries and steering Glamorgan towards a 400 total against Kent; at Brooklands race track, Weybridge, Earl Howe was seriously injured when his car overturned.

At Stockton-on-Tees Mr. Hore-Belisha stated that in eight years the number of cars on Britain's roads had doubled and was increasing by 500 daily; an Australian airman called Broadbent touched down at Karachi in an attempt to break the record for a solo flight to England.

At Wembley Stadium, after 14 years, the traditional last Saturday in April for the Cup Final had been abandoned in favour of the fifth month of the year to mark the Coronation celebrations.

King George VI and Queen Elizabeth saw the match between Sunderland and Preston.

It was an intriguing final for neither club had previously appeared at Wembley. Preston had last appeared in the final in 1922 when they lost by the only goal to Huddersfield Town at Stamford Bridge.

Sunderland's only previous appearance at this ultimate stage had been in 1913 when they lost to Aston Villa, also by the only goal scored. Neither side had any League problems, Sunderland finishing 8th in the First Division and Preston 14th.

This appeared to give Sunderland the edge, but Cup form suggested Preston. The Lancashire team had won all their ties with a goal average of 19 against 6.

The luck of the draw had favoured them in the early rounds. Newcastle United went to Deepdale and lost 0-2. Stoke City followed and were thrashed 1-5. In Round Five Preston, although at home once more, got their closest call on their way to Wembley, against Exeter City, who had to apply for re-election to the Third (South) that season.

Preston got through 5-3, but at one stage were losing 2-3 and were held until the last quarter-of-an-hour.

Preston showed this was an isolated lapse of form for they then went to White Hart Lane and mopped up Spurs 3-1, followed by a convincing 4-1 success over West Bromwich Albion at Highbury in the semi-final.

Sunderland had needed eight matches to get to Wembley. They beat Southampton at The Dell 3-2, but Third Division Luton Town, led by Joe Payne, held them 2-2 at Kenilworth Road.

Sunderland took the replay at Roker Park comfortably, 3-1, as they did Swansea Town 3-0 in Round Five.

Then many on Wearside thought their chance was gone when they were held 1-1 by the Wolves, but they drew 2-2 after extra time at Molineux and in the second replay at Hillsborough turned in their best performance of the season, winning 4-0.

Betting, tradition with Preston

In the semi-final they were given another fright, by Millwall, who that season had made history by becoming the first team from the Third Division to reach the semi-final of the F.A. Cup.

Millwall took a quick lead and Sunderland just scraped through by the odd goal of three.

Sunderland were able to field a full-strength side for the final, their right-half, Thomson, recovering from a knee injury in good time.

Preston had a more serious problem. Their first choice goalkeeper, international Harry Holdcroft, had missed the semi-final through injury. He was now fit again but North End decided to keep Mick Burns in goal.

The last minute betting favoured Preston who also had tradition on their side. This was their fifth final, and Sunderland's second, and in Frank O'Donnell—who had scored in every round—they had the man many considered to be the best centre-forward in Britain at the time.

The critics were not sure. They conceded O'Donnell could be the match-winner but they were mindful of Sunderland's Raich Carter. *It was a perfect,*

Raich Carter's goal 'fit to set before the Queen ...'

early summer day and to honour the new King there were massed bands from Chatham, Portsmouth and the Irish Guards. A formation of R.A.F. planes flew overhead. There were exactly 28 months of peace and the old way of life left to us before Germany marched against Poland.

A hash of a glorious pass

From the start and for much of the first half things ran strongly in Preston's favour and up to this moment there was a tradition that the side who scored first at Wembley won the Cup. This had been so in 12 of the previous 14 Wembley finals.

So, the first goal meant far more even

the home-town genius, who put Sunderland ahead for the first time with 19 minutes left.

Carter had a swerve that was doubly deceptive — it was not always as pronounced as it appeared to be but it was invariably faster than it looked.

In the 71st minute, Carter scored a goal fit to lay before his new Queen.

He dribbled—it was not a dirty word in football then—drew Gallimore, beat him, took on Tremelling, beat him as well and cracked a low shot past Burns.

Six minutes later it was all over. There was a stoppage while Gurney received attention from his trainer. The referee restarted play with a dropped ball, Sunderland got possession and were through with the best combined move of the game.

Gurney, to Gallacher to Burbanks, a short dribble, a sharply angled shot— and the net behind Burns was alive for the third time.

There were 93,000 —utterly silent

It ended as Sunderland 3, Preston North End 1, and Horatio Carter, bred-and-born in Sunderland, experienced that kind of timeless moment vouchsafed to few mortals when he received the Cup from the hands of The Queen.

In those days they did not do a lap of honour, with the Cup, its lid and its plinth being waved before wildly cheering sections of the crowd.

Carter held the whole thing carefully aloft, two of his team mates hoisted their captain on to their shoulders and solemnly headed for the dressing room.

Suddenly, the mass bands struck up the National Anthem. Carefully, Carter and his precious burden were put down. He stood, an unconsciously dramatic figure against the background of 93,000 spectators—all utterly silent.

After the last notes, Carter went up on to his consorts' shoulders again and the multitude stood quite happily behind the barriers and watched captain and cup borne away out of sight.

It might stir further memories of that day, a generation ago, to give the teams: They were: **Sunderland** — Mapson; Gorman, Hall; Thomson, Johnston, McNab; Duns, Carter, Gurney, Gallacher, Burbanks.

Preston — Burns; Gallimore, Beattie; Shankly, Tremelling, Milne; Dougal, Beresford, O'Donnell (F), Fagan, O'Donnell (H).

---

than it does these days, in the context of this particular match, and it was always odds on that Preston would get it.

Bob Gurney made a hash of the first big chance. Carter put him through with a glorious pass but the centre-forward, from penalty spot range, lifted it over the bar.

Preston kept the edge and seven minutes from half-time Frank O'Donnell joined the select band who have scored in every round of the Cup.

Played them out of sight

Dougal, the outside-right, worked the ball into the middle and the big centre-forward switched to the right flank. At just the right moment, Dougal passed to O'Donnell and, taking the ball forward a few yards, he put a beauty past Mapson.

That was how it stood at half time, but then Sunderland—League champions the previous season—did what no other team had done before them quite so con-

Carter is chaired off by Len Duns and Sandy McNab. Jimmy Gorman is on the left.

vincingly . . . they came from behind against fit, cock-a-hoop opponents and played them out of sight.

They needed a quick equaliser to put them back in the game—and they got it. Burbanks forced a corner, took it himself, and after one header had gone astray Gurney beat Burns with a second go and it was 1-1 and all to play for.

Carter, showing that even the greatest players are always prone to error, passed when he had the goal at his mercy, but there was no mistaking Sunderland's quality in the second half.

They opened up the game and the Preston backs had difficulty in dealing with wingers Duns and Burbanks.

Gurney's constant interchange with Duns to escape Tremelling added to North End's problems, but it was Carter,

CHARLES BUCHAN'S

FOOTBALL MONTHLY

MARCH, 1967

2/6

JIM BAXTER
Sunderland

"THE MEN FROM ROKER"

GEORGE MULHALL

JOHN O'HARE

NEIL MARTIN

WILLIAM HUGHES

An early Sunderland attack is thwarted by Wright, the Everton full-back.

Neil Martin, the Sunderland centre-forward, bravely challenges the Everton keeper West

John O'Hare lunges, but just can't make contact.

... THE CHARLES BUCHAN CAMERA RECENTLY VISITED ROKER PARK FOR THE SUNDERLAND VERSUS EVERTON CLASH...

Season 1967-68 started slightly better than of late, before quickly following the recent usual pattern, of a slide down the table and a fight against relegation. There was a glimmer of hope in the form of youth international Colin Suggett and the emergence of Colin Todd, but despite this, McColl still felt the need to bolster his squad with a couple of old heads.

One player considered surplus to requirements was Jim Baxter, after one indiscretion too many. The club were basically prepared to release him, but to their astonishment, Nottingham Forest came in with a £100,000 offer, on the basis of a good performance by the player against them earlier in the season. Sunderland couldn't wait to get rid. However, within 18 months Nottingham Forest had released the player on a free transfer, after he failed to live up to their high hopes.

By the end of January, the club had been knocked out of the F.A. Cup by Norwich, and were down in 19th place, and next up was a trip to high flying Sheffield Wednesday, managed by Alan Brown of course.

Despite a 1-0 win, McColl was summoned to a meeting with the board, and told his services were no longer needed. Of course, there was lots of speculation about who might be the next incumbent, but during a press conference, Ian McColl inadvertently let the cat out of the bag, when he revealed that his successor would be...Alan Brown.

As the new manager was preparing to take over, the club was dispensing with the services of just the type of player he would surely need. Neil Martin had joined at the same time as Jim Baxter, but without the fanfare. He made a far greater impression on the team and supporters,

and although tough and uncompromising, he had a good touch, and his record of 46 goals in 99 appearances is exceptional, especially when you consider the type of football Sunderland served up. The club received double what they had paid for him, when he was allowed to join fellow relegation candidates Coventry City.

Solid pragmatic performances followed Brown's appointment, with an unflashy 15th place finish, followed by a 17th place the next season.

However the manager wasted precious resources on players such as Joe Baker, who had never recovered from an injury sustained at Nottingham Forest and Calvin Palmer from Stoke. These signings had been financed by the sale of Colin Suggett to West Brom, and without him they only managed a feeble 30 league goals! The quality of the football on offer was so poor, it was little wonder that fans were staying away from Roker Park.

After beginning the 1969-70 campaign poorly, they were in the relegation zone virtually all season, spending only one week outside it, before they timidly returned to Division Two. The manager had certain players that he obviously didn't rate, such as Porterfield and Palmer, and even though results were terrible, they were never given a chance to help the team.

It had taken six years to return last time, how long would it take now? The changing face of football finances threatened to leave Sunderland far behind. Decreasing crowd numbers affected the bank balance, and the modern players were far more attracted to London, or the soccer hotspots of Manchester or Liverpool than they had been in the past. The country was also to enter a

period of economic instability that would disproportionately affect the North of England.

Alan Brown was his usual bombastic self: 'This is only a blip. A temporary set-back, we have already laid the foundations for a successful team.' In a perverse way he was proved right, but not with him at the helm, and although it cannot be doubted that he had the best interests of the club at heart, they had suffered the only two relegations of their history on his watch.

There were only 16,000 inside Roker Park for the first home game back in Division Two against Watford, and despite being entertained by a 3-3 draw, this figure had dropped to 11,000 by the next home game. Only a big crowd for the Middlesbrough derby broke the cycle.

Somehow, the board found the money to finance another big signing. Dave Watson of Rotherham, could play centre half or centre forward. Alan Brown saw him as a forward, but it was not until he played regularly as a defender that he discovered his best form.

Fans just couldn't wait for the season to end, a mediocre 13th place and apathy all round. Birmingham City provided the opposition for the opening game of the 1971-72 season, and there were less than 10,000 there to see it, the sort of figure the reserves used to play in front of! In a sign that there was quality within the side, an early season line-up contained eight players who would be in the victorious Cup team less than two years later. But the manager just couldn't make it click.

Even though they improved to finish fifth, the fans didn't return, they were never convinced that promotion was a real possibility.

The next season proved to be the end for Alan Brown. He couldn't complain that he hadn't been backed by the club, but enough was enough, things couldn't be allowed to slide for much longer.

The axe finally fell in October 1972, and initially, first team coach Billy Elliott took caretaker charge. One of the first things he did was to move Dave Watson back to centre half, and when Bob Stokoe arrived as manager, he agreed with the decision, and the player began to settle in the position to which he was best suited.

Bob Stokoe was to become a legend on Wearside. Not bad for someone who had crossed the Tyne/Wear divide, but they were different times back then, the rivalry might have been fierce, but there was not the same sort of visceral hatred that exists today.

Stokoe had taken a long and winding road to arrive at his first big managerial job, via Bury, Charlton, Rochdale, Carlisle and Blackpool, and though considered an honest and decent man, there was little on his C.V. that suggested the immediate impact he was to have.

Gradually the League form improved, but it was in the F.A. Cup that Sunderland grabbed the football world's attention. A low key start, beating Notts County 2-0 after a replay, watched by an above average 30,000. It then took another replay to dispose of Division Four Reading, before their biggest task to date, and a trip to Maine Road to take on Manchester City.

By then, Stokoe had dipped his toe in the transfer market with a couple of low key, but astute signings. First he picked up full back Ron Guthrie from Newcastle United, and then brought in centre forward Vic Halom from LutonTown. Halom was not a prolific scorer, but his work rate was to fit in perfectly with the team ethos, and he soon became a fan's favourite.

Backed by a massive following, Sunderland held Manchester City to a draw, before beating them back at Wearside on a night of raw passion. Halom set up the victory, after lashing home a blockbuster from a tight angle, before Billy Hughes bagged the others in a 3-1 victory.

With a home tie next up against Luton Town, the fans began to dream of a trip to the Twin Towers, but Luton provided stern opposition, and it took a late Guthrie effort to finally kill them off, in a 2-0 win.

With a semi-final against Arsenal at Hillsborough to look forward to, it was essential that the players maintained their League form to avoid being dragged into a relegation dogfight. In the end, there were to be no worries on that score, as the confidence gained from their cup exploits enabled them to move up the table.

They were clear underdog's for the Arsenal game. The Gunners were a fine team who had reached the Cup Final for the two previous seasons, but roared on by a passionate crowd, the Sunderland players once more raised their game, to run out worthy 2-1 winners at Hillsborough.

The final turned out to be a memorable occasion. The tone for the day was set when the T.V. cameras were allowed to accompany the Sunderland players on their bus to the

stadium, and then capture the Sunderland players revelling in the atmosphere, waving to friends and family in the crowd. By contrast Leeds looked sullen and nervous, after all, they were the overwhelming favourites, but also with a history of choking when the going got tough.

Sunderland had a game plan, a resolute defence with the potential for a quick counter attack. And when they took a 32nd minute lead through Ian Porterfield, they could exploit this strategy to the full.

Wave after wave came at the Sunderland goal, all of them repulsed, but it still took one extra bit of magic from Jim Montgomery in the Sunderland goal, to ensure the trophy was heading back to Wearside, as he somehow turned Peter Lorimer's piledriver onto the bar.

The final whistle saw euphoric scenes, and the never to be forgotten image of of Bob Stokoe dancing across the Wembley turf waving his trilby hat in the air as he dashed to embrace his players.

The year of 1973 was destined to pass in to folklore and the history of Sunderland Football Club. A time when the football supporters of Wearside fell in love with their team once more. However, despite this, it would still be another three seasons before Sunderland returned to the top flight, by which time, many of those Wembley heroes would have moved on.

GEORGE KINNELL

DEREK FORSTER

ROBERT KERR

CECIL IRWIN

It was a long way round to join his cousin — but GEORGE KINNELL

OF SUNDERLAND

'made' it

GEORGE KINNELL, a lean, lantern-jawed Scot, had to travel from his native Aberdeen via the Potteries and Lancashire to join his cousin, Jim Baxter, at Sunderland. And a remarkable story lies behind the route he took.

George came south of the Border when Stoke City forked out the handsome sum of £30,000 to Aberdeen for the services of this talented half-back. He could play at wing-half or centre-half, and it was for his ability as pivot that City signed him.

On the Saturday he played for Aberdeen, and on the Monday he was a Stoke player. It was as swift and simple as that.

But as the months went by at Stoke, George, who had proved his versatility at centre-half, wing-half and inside-forward, found that regular first-team football was becoming more and more a thing of the past. And towards the end of last season, it was plain that the parting of the ways for club and player was close at hand.

Sunderland, for whom Jim Baxter had become a drawing card—£70,000 or so changed hands—were showing some interest in George. But their interest never materialised into a concrete offer.

Came the close season, and Stoke were once more involved in the business of trying to sign a centre-half—this time Mike England, the Welsh international starring with Blackburn Rovers. Stoke were ready to offer Blackburn cash and players for England. And George Kinnell was one of the players.

The trouble was that the players Blackburn DID want were the players Stoke DIDN'T want to let go . . . and so England moved to Tottenham in a straight £95,000 cash deal. Sunderland and Blackburn had had their chance, and neither club had taken it.

But a former Stoke player who had moved on — Jimmy McIlroy, now managing Oldham — hadn't forgotten about George Kinnell. Jimmy went back to Stoke and paid out £25,000 for a "package deal" which took George and winger Keith Bebbington to Boundary Park. I'm told on good authority that Bebbington was rated at around £17,000 in that deal.

Then things began to happen—fast. George Kinnell was chosen at inside-forward for Oldham, as the Lancashire club set about the business of trying to win a place in the Second Division.

Meantime, Sunderland were quietly sliding down the First Division, and they had centre-half star Charlie Hurley out of action through injury . . . while Blackburn, after kicking off in the Second Division as though they were going to bounce straight back to the First, were finding the going tough.

And in his new role for Oldham, George Kinnell was banging in the goals at a rate which any centre-forward in Britain would have been proud to claim.

Suddenly, Blackburn and Sunderland decided that what they needed was George Kinnell, to prop up their respective defences. Suddenly, the bargain-buy from Stoke became a wanted man . . . wanted by the clubs who could have bought him straight from City months earlier. Blackburn, in fact, could have had Kinnell, and at least one other City player AND cash for Mike England.

Now Jimmy McIlroy was telling Sunderland that he DIDN'T want to let George go . . . unless a proposed player-exchange deal satisfied him that it would be good business for Oldham.

And Blackburn? THEY were ready to trade in exchange George Jones, their £30,000 inside-forward buy from Bury who had since re-joined that club.

In the end, Oldham turned down the Blackburn proposition; and they decided that Sunderland's idea of a deal was not the answer, either. So it looked as if George Kinnell's hopes of a return to higher grade Soccer depended upon Oldham's promotion aspirations being achieved at the end of the season.

But, finally, George was able to make Oldham see HIS point of view . . . and Athletic bowed to his wishes. "It was no use making George stay, if it meant that he wasn't going to be happy," said Jimmy McIlroy. "That would have been of little use to him—or us."

So, on a Saturday morning in October, George Kinnell met Sunderland officials, and played his last game for Oldham the same afternoon. It was a game neither he nor the fans will forget in a hurry. He missed a penalty, scored another from the spot, and inspired Athletic to a 6-2 trouncing of Walsall.

A few days later, he signed for Sunderland, and Oldham made an acknowledged 140 per cent. profit on the deal, which, by my reckoning, means they pocketed a cheque for almost £20,000.

On the night of Tuesday, October 25, George Kinnell made his bow for Sunderland at centre-half against his *first* English club, Stoke City, then sitting at the top of the First Division. And no-one could have gained more satisfaction from the result—Sunderland 2, Stoke 1.

DAVE PARKER

George Kinnell
Sunderland

Sunderland goalkeeper Jim Montgomery dives to save

SUNDERLAND:

Back row — Montgomery, Ashurst, Todd, Baxter, Kerr, Forster; Centre row — Heslop, Suggett, Gauden, Hughes, Shoulder, Irwin, Hurley; Front row — Harvey, Kinnell, Mulhall, O'Hare (now Derby), Parke, Herd, Martin.

COLIN SUGGETT

SUNDERLAND'S INSIDE FORWARD

Talks about his hopes for the future

"I WANT TO PLAY FOR ENGLAND"

I come from a footballing family, my two brothers play soccer as well as myself, although they are members of local teams. My younger brother, Alan, in fact is only seventeen and still at school, has already been a magnet for three clubs, although to be honest, I don't think he will take up professional football.

But there was no doubt in my mind what I wanted to be when I left school. It was professional football all the way. I stayed on at school until I was sixteen so that I could take my G.C.E's, I managed four passes, but a year before I left, I had already taken half the plunge. For I had signed amateur forms for Sunderland. Next Christmas, I'll celebrate my twenty-first birthday…so that I reckon that by then I will be able to say I've gained plenty of experience in top-class soccer.

They used to say about the North East that if you shouted down a coal-mine, up would come a footballer. Well, plenty of top-class players have graced the game from our area and I hope that my name will be linked with the best as years go by.

I was born in Washington, County Durham of course! And, like my Roker team-mate, Colin Todd, who is the same age as myself, to within a few days, I played for Chester-le-Street schoolboys. I graduated to Durham and England boys, and the county team reached the final of the English Schools Shield, before losing 3-2 to Erdington from Birmingham. So I learned pretty soon in life what disappointments there can be in football, as well as the high-spots.

In fact, I can recall another occasion when I walked off the park feeling choked, that was

in a game against Nottingham Forest last season. We lost 1-0 and I was kicking myself for missing an open goal.

Goals, you see, are what matter to me. I started out in schoolboy football as a right-winger, but I have switched inside now and I consider that my role is to get goals, the more the better.

I now regard myself as a striker, even though at 5 feet 8 inches, I'm no giant, but I am a solid 11st.

I made my Football League debut for Sunderland early in 1966 and it wasn't exactly a happy one, we lost 3-0 at Stoke. But I must have confirmed the good impression of the soccer judges, because by the following season, I had established myself in the first-team, in fact I played in all 42 league games.

The most memorable game was the one we played at Old Trafford against the mighty Manchester United, a game which was important to us, because we still needed points to ensure our First Division status. It was the final match of the season and it was just as vital to United, for victory over us could give them the League Championship.

United's great rivals Manchester City, were up at St James's Park, trying to win there and pip the Busby boys for the title. City won a dramatic game 4-3, but it wasn't quite so tight in the end, for down at Old Trafford, Sunderland were doing the unexpected and winning. Manchester United managed to score, but we put two past them. I scored one and made the other goal and it's a memory which will live with me always.

Obviously, the game in which I love to play is the local derby against Newcastle. Ever since I can remember, these two teams have had old scores to settle and the fanatacism of the rival

supporters takes some beating. Believe me, there's nothing a Sunderland player likes better than to walk off the pitch at the end of a derby duel knowing he's helped to put one across the old enemy.

Now, I don't pretend to know all the answers in this game, you are always learning and there is always someone who can teach you a trick or two, not to mention the odd lesson! But every footballer worth his salt must have ambitions and I have mine.

I gained England youth honours, at amateur and apprentice level and so it's only natural that I should hope to carry on where I left off there… by being awarded an England Under 23 cap, and graduating eventually to the full international team. I'm not being big-headed when I say this, merely stating an ambition.

The other ambition I have is to go to Wembley with Sunderland in the F.A. Cup Final. Sunderland haven't exactly pulled up any trees in recent years, but there is a fair way to go before I need to start thinking about hanging up my boots. And some time during my career, I aim to be a member of a Sunderland Cup winning team. I think we have a pretty fair chance too, for we are now holding our own in the First Division and we are proving increasingly hard to beat. We have a good leavening experience and youth and there is plenty of ability in our line-up.

One day, perhaps this coming season, Sunderland will take the F.A. Cup back to Roker and when they do, I aim to be there with them. Goals are my gimmick, so I hope to help shoot Sunderland to that final at Wembley.

GAIN STRENGTH! PERSONALITY! MUSCLES!

Build yourself a FANTASTIC BODY! A perfect book COMPLETELY ILLUSTRATED will give you a FABULOUS PHYSIQUE of the GYMNAST or the ATHLETE in a FEW WEEKS. All this WITHOUT ANY ADDITIONAL EXPENSE WHATSOEVER. Do it in the PRIVACY of your home and come out a COMPLETELY NEW MAN. Money refunded within seven days if not delighted. New GREAT exercises for one of the FASTEST Body Building Courses in commerce.

ONLY 20s. 0d. $3 Post Free
SERPER STRENGTH COMPANY
(FM) 41 Clabon Mews, London, S.W.1

BOYS SOCCER SETS

Ideal gift for young soccer players containing coloured jersey, shorts & stretch nylon socks. State colours, chest, waist and shoe size.

Waist: 24" 29/6, 26/28" 30/-, 30/32" 31/6, Glasgow Celtic 28" 34/6, 32" 37/6, 34" 40/-.

Please include 3/- p. & p. with P.O. for above. Supplies of Adidas, Mitre, George Best & Puma FOOTBALL BOOTS also available, nylon & cotton TRACK SUITS from 29/11 upwards.

Send type & size required for price quotation.

Can supply all sports equipment for senior teams.

Send P.O. to:

CARDIFF SPORTSGEAR
194 WHITCHURCH RD., CARDIFF. TEL. 34442.

---

800 FOOTBALL BOOTS
at less than HALF PRICE

5-Star Slazenger (sizes 6, 11, 11½ & 12)	Usually £6-5-0	OUR PRICE	45/-
3-Star (Red) (sizes 6, 11, 11½ & 12)	Usually £4-5-0	OUR PRICE	40/-
1-Star (sizes 6, 9½, 10, 10½, 11 & 12)	Usually £2-19-11		35/-

C.W.O. plus 4/6 p. & p. on all pairs

S. S. MOORE
22 Arthur Street, BELFAST, N. Ireland

DON'T BE BULLIED

Get tough double quick. Morley LIGHTNING QUICK Ju-Jitsu Course shows how. Make any attacker helpless in a flash—with your BARE HANDS. Easy to learn; quick Jap combat tricks and all knock-out blows. Fear no one. Full 48-lesson course Only 10/- post paid.

BODY-BUILDING

Powerful Arms Course, 3/6; Powerful Chest Course, 3/6; Muscular Legs Course, 3/6; Powerful Abdomen, 3/6. (All Four 12/6.) Tricks of Self Defence and How To Do Them. 4/6 post paid. How to Conquer Nervous Fears, 4/6. Natural Way To Gain Weight, 4/6. Manual of Karate, 20/-.

J. J. MORLEY (F.M.22)
28 Dean Road, London, N.W.2

MANUFACTURERS OF
FOOTBALL RUGBY JERSEYS & TRACK SUITS

Plain striped and circlet designs, Shorts, Stockings, etc.

SPEEDY DELIVERY
NEWTON SPORTSWEAR
17 Market Street
Denton, Nr. M/C.
DEN 2583

SUPPLIED IN TEAM SETS ONLY
Price list on request

SUPPORTERS SHOULDER BAGS 21/6 p/p 3/-

Attractively made in strong waterproof canvas with adjustable shoulder strap. Made in club colours, with team emblem on the side. Ideal for carrying football gear or for general use as an everyday holdall. Available in most 1st Division clubs and leading Scottish teams.

J. W. RAMSBOTHAM (DEPT. FM10) 393 Fore Street, Edmonton, London, N.9

FOOTBALL BOOTS
FROM 26/6

Make this your happiest Christmas ever with a pair of Pocock or Gola football boots. Sturdy, hardwearing and comfortable. Leather uppers with moulded multi-studded soles.
Boys size 7-10 26/6   Youths size 2-5 31/-
Boys size 11-1 28/-   Mens size 6-12 52/6
P & P all orders 2/6
Make sure of yours now

Dept. B.2 P & I MAIL ORDER LTD.
120 Aigburth Road, Liverpool, 17

BENNETTS SPORTS LTD

Largest range of Football equipment, clothing, etc., in the area. Special terms for clubs.

NEW! FOOTBALL KIT PACKS
from 34/- each plus 2/6 p.p.

Supplied in most league club colours to your requirements. Each pack contains: Jersey, shorts and socks. Drop us a line together with s.a.e. stating your chest, waist and shoe size. Q.P.R. Jersey—please allow 10/- extra.

NEW! FOOTBALL BOOTS
from 37/6 upwards
Boys' .. from size 7 (small)
Men's .. up to size 12
S.a.e. for further details

13 RUISLIP ROAD, GREENFORD, MIDDX.
Tel.: WAX 6211

BE TALLER

in 12 days or **money back.** New gland and spinal discovery increases height 2 to 5 inches. "I have gained 4½ inches" —P.D. "I have gained 3½ inches"—R.O. Imposing height will enable you to forge ahead on the high road of splendid success. Guaranteed harmless. Full course 10/- (or $1.50). Air Mail 15/-. Details 2d. Sent under plain cover.

JOHN H. MORLEY (F.M.22)
28 Dean Road, London, NW2

KICK OFF IN STYLE
Junior FOOTBALL OUTFIT
FROM 26/6

Authentic kits available in all 1st Division clubs and leading Scottish teams. Consisting of Jersey, Shorts, Socks, Team Badge, **AND NOW NUMERAL AND STAR PHOTOGRAPH INCLUDED AT NO EXTRA CHARGE.** All clothing made by top English manufacturers UMBRO and UWIN who kit the actual clubs.

CHEST	22"	24"	26"-28"	30"	32"	34"	36"-38"
	26/6	29/6	32/6	34/6	36/6	39/6	42/6

Post & packaging 3/-. Teams with striped shirts 4/- extra.

WHAT A GAME!
ALL THE THRILLS & EXCITEMENT OF PROFESSIONAL SOCCER
ALL IN THE BRAND NEW SOCCERAMA

Be your own team manager with this unique soccerama game. Fight your way up the divisions, buy and sell players. Compete for the F.A. and European Cups avoiding penalties and fines. Keeps the family amused for hours. (2 to 6 players.) Ideal Xmas gift. Complete with colourful 22 x 15 in. Board, Dice, Money, etc. Money back guarantee. Send cash, P.O. or cheque now, to:

29/11 POST & PACKING 2/-

IMPEX SALES & SUPPLY, DEPT. "G"
7 Warstone Parade East, Birmingham 18

GUITARS, AMPLIFIERS AND ACCESSORIES

72 PAGE GUITAR CATALOGUE FREE

Just off the press—72 pages packed full of details and pictures of all types and makes of Guitars, Pickups Amplifiers, Echo-units, Microphones, Accessories, etc. Wonderful cash bargains or easy terms. Call or write for your FREE copy today.

BELL MUSIC (Dept. 21).
157-159 Ewell Road, SURBITON, Surrey.
Callers welcome. Open all day Saturday.

CLUB JACKETS
BUY BRITISH

- As worn and approved by Leading Clubs—ideal for Supporters too.

- Distinctive for those who want a 'cut above' the usual jacket.

- Smart enough to be worn anywhere, any time.

JET BLACK NYLON with **QUILTED** GOLD lining or MIDNIGHT BLUE with RED LINING.

Sizes: 34"–42"

Yours for ONLY

49/11 Plus 3/6 p & p.

State chest size and colour choice.

COMMAND SURPLUS CENTRE LTD (FM19)
132 Wandsworth High Street, London SW18

SUNDERLAND

HERE is the senior squad with which hopes to put Sunderland back at the
Roker Park manager Alan Brown top of the soccer tree:

BACK: Cecil Irwin, Colin Todd, Charlie Hurley, Jim Montgomery,
Colin Suggett, Len Ashurst, John Porterfield

FRONT ROW: Gordon Harris, George Kinnell, George Mulhall,
Calvin Palmer, George Herd, Martin Harvey, Bruce Stuckey

COLIN SUGGETT
Sunderland

AMBITION? A SCOTTISH CAP

HIS manager, Alan Brown, reckons that Sunderland's Bobby Park will be playing in an international at Wembley by 1974. That would still only make the young Scot a mere 22.

Perhaps the most remarkable thing about Mr Brown's prediction is that it was made of a 17-year-old who, at that time, had yet to kick a ball in a League match.

An hour or so later, Bobby did get on to the pitch as a substitute against Crystal Palace for Calvin Palmer.

His full League debut, however, was on October 11, 1969, and it was hardly an easy first game. Sunderland's opponents were Everton, the ground was Goodison Park and the home team ran out 3-1 winners.

His first goal came in a 2-1 home win against Ipswich

and his second, again at Roker Park, against Newcastle United, although there was some dispute between Bobby and Dennis Tueart as to who actually put the finishing touches to that one.

In his first full season he had a run of 26 First Division appearances for the club only to see Sunderland relegated to the Second Division.

"To be honest," says Bobby, "the Second Division is tough—the quick and the dead sort of stuff—but I was satisfied with my form until I got a shin injury last November."

There is quite a Scottish contingent at Roker Park to make Bobby feel at home. He was born in Coatbridge and played at left-half at school, preferring a mid-field role. His father had been a professional footballer with St. Mirren and he had always wanted to follow in his footsteps.

When a Sunderland scout spotted him he jumped at the chance to join the club. Bobby admits that as a lad he was an admirer of the great Jim Baxter, and started out by trying to copy his style.

"As I got older, however, I realised it would better for me to stick to my natural style," he says. "I think all young players have the same hopes and ambitions, and mine are to play for Scotland and be a success in a good club team. I've played for the Scottish Youth side and the next step will be an Under-23 cap."

Bobby rates Everton's Alan Ball as the most difficult player he has faced so far. "He never stops moving and he's world class into the bargain," he explains.

He says, however, that the player he admires most is Bobby Charlton. He makes the choice because of Charlton's total dedication to the game, as well as for the example he sets to all other players on the field.

**Everton's Allan Ball —
always on the move.**

**Bobby Park, Sunderland's
Scottish half-back**

WILLIAM
HUGHES
Sunderland

JOHN
ROBERTS
Arsenal

SUNDERLAND DUET
Martin Harvey and Gordon Harris

DENNIS
TUEART
Sunderland

COLIN
TODD
Sunderland

JOE BAKER
Sunderland

COLIN TODD
Sunderland

£10.00 FOR M

Every Game I Played In Was Worth £500 To My Old Club...

I can still hear my grandmother calling out from the doorway of the house in Cowdenbeath where I lived with her: "Come in and do your lessons."

But, at 12 years of age, I was too busy at lessons I liked a bit better, learning to shoot and dribble and control a wee rubber ball in the streets of the Fife mining town.

Now it seems I really profited from these street lessons. For I am playing for Sunderland. I've got money in the bank, and invested. I drive a big car. I live in a beautiful house and every time I go out, somebody stops to wish me well. Money has loomed large for me in football, but I don't consider myself all that money conscious. For instance…

I was transferred to Sunderland from Raith Rovers for £35,000. Part of the deal was that, after I had played 20 league games for my new club, another £10,000 would go to the one I left. As I stood to get a percentage of the addition to the fee, you might think I'd be counting the games as they went by.

Know what? I didn't even notice the passing of the 20th game, somebody had to tell me I was now a £45,000 player.

Yet the whole story could have been entirely different. I might have gone straight from school to Leeds United when I was 15. I might have gone to Hearts when I was 17. I nearly went to Celtic when I was 18. And West Bromwich Albion and Rangers all watched me regularly when I was with Raith Rovers.

The man who really set me on the trail to the top in football was another Fifer called Andy Young. He ran the Lochore Welfare junior club and was a scout for Celtic, for whom he used to play.

At this time, Andy was sending a lot of youngsters to Parkhead. I wondered why he didn't send me, eventually I asked. I will never forget the advice I got. It was, "If you go there just now, you might easily get lost among Celtic's big crowd of young hopefuls. You have got a great future in the game, but only if you go to a club where your influence will be felt in the first-team.

I could hardly believe him, but after thinking over what he said , I went along with it. Telling myself I'd better watch out I didn't get a big head.

And still the scouts kept coming. Among them Rangers, Hearts, West Bromwich, East

Don't Delay!

"Get him! He's trying to get in before us for a copy of FOOTBALL MONTHLY!"

JACKPOT OLD CLUB

Fife, Everton, Liverpool, Southend and Raith Rovers. I played trials for Hearts and East Fife. Then one day, George Farm, manager of Raith Rovers, now manager of Dunfermline. Mr Farm is one of these direct-action men. He soon had me convinced that I should sign for Rovers. And I did.

• • • • • • • • • • • • •

played badly he wasn't long in letting you know all about it. And how he could lay it on the line. Still, I always liked his approach.

Although I have had only two senior clubs, there have been four managers in my life. George Farm who took Raith to promotion; Tommy Walker who succeeded him, and is one of the kind of bosses it's impossible not to like; Ian McColl, who brought me to Sunderland and gave me my big chance; and Alan Brown, who took over at Roker Park almost two years ago.

There have been many fantastic stories about the iron discipline of Mr Brown. He is supposed to be the toughest boss in Britain. I would like to say that he is the fairest.

When he came to Roker Park he immediately dropped me. I was out of the team for a long time too. Naturally I began to think I wasn't his type of player, that I had no future at Sunderland.

So I made for his office, feeling pretty sore. Mr Brown came back quickly when I asked him: "Am I out of the side because I am not your type of player?"

I was partly right at that.

The boss told me that I had to learn to defend as well as attack. He felt there was no room in the tough First Division for a player who only waited for the ball and then set out to create goal chances.

That must certainly be part of my make-up, he said, but I must also learn to tackle and work in defence. He finished by telling me I could become the greatest attacking wing-half in England, but I must be ready and willing to defend.

I walked out of his office and went back to the reserves, determined to improve my tackling and covering.

And it wasn't long before I was back in the first team.

No, the boss isn't really tough, he's just ruthlessly honest about each individual's strengths and weaknesses.

Maybe you've heard me described as a 'second Jim Baxter.' It's often been said I look like him and play like him.

This comparison is something I have had to live with since I signed for Raith Rovers, and I hate it!

Don't get me wrong, I think Baxter is one of the top players ever to come out of Scotland, but I don't want to be compared with any player.

I am Ian Porterfield, not Jim Baxter the second. You see, I followed Jim at Raith Rovers and I followed him at Sunderland. We both come

from Cowdenbeath and we are both wing-half backs who like to go on the attack.

I have often been told that, in his early days at Kirkaldy, Baxter was also accused of paying too much attention to attack and too little to defence.

But if that is your natural game, it's very difficult to get rid of the ball.

And so, when I became a Sunderland player, the cry went up, 'He's the new Jim Baxter.'

Do you know, whenever I meet Jim I can feel this 'something' between us. It's a strange sort of feeling.

But I might never have followed the same path as Baxter if things hadn't taken that different turning when I was 15. When Leeds United came on the scene.

And that really was one out of the blue.

Mr Don Revie, then a coach with Leeds United, had come up to Cowdenbeath to visit relations. They owned a shop my mother often used.

She was in the shop with a neighbour when the lady behind the counter started talking about Mr Revie's visit.

My mother's friend casually said: "Why don't you tell him about Mrs Porterfield's son, Ian? The lad sis always playing football."

Next thing I knew Mr Revie asked me to come out and show him what I could do on a nearby pitch.

For half an hour he put me through a non-stop work-out. I took shots at him in goal. I dribbled against him.

He put in some tough tackles on me, then he asked if I would like to come down to Leeds.

So I went to Elland Road, but very quickly became homesick and came back to Cowdenbeath. And then everything started up again…

"Don't be upset—after all there are girls' football teams!"

GORDON
HARRIS
Sunderland

Sunderland A.F.C. 1970

BACK ROW:
Richie Pitt, Colin Symm, Gordon Harris, Jimmy Montgomery, Len Ashurst, Martin Harvey, Brian Heslop

FRONT ROW:
Billy Hughes, Dennis Tueart, Calvin Palmer, Colin Todd, Joe Baker, Ian Porterfield, Bobby Kerr

This is the story behind one club's admission that times are not what they were and their willingness to face up to the hard facts in an area where the game has temporarily lost much of its appeal. PETER MORRIS tells here of the mood and the men he met going round SUNDERLAND. There are other towns and cities where the pinch of failure has been felt even more acutely. These then are our findings from this special inquiry into the areas. . . .

WHERE SOCCER HAS GONE SOUR

CHARLES BUCHAN'S **FOOTBALL** MONTHLY

ibpa

FOUNDED IN 1951
BY CHARLES BUCHAN
CAPTAIN OF SUNDERLAND.
ARSENAL AND ENGLAND

DECEMBER, 1970 No. 232

EDITOR   PAT COLLINS   ART EDITOR
                                          REGINALD BASS
ASSISTANT EDITORS
          MALCOLM CUMMING   ADVERTISEMENT MANAGER
                PETER MORRIS   G. A. IRELAND

COVER-POINT
Bob Wilson
(ARSENAL)
covers a neat
miss.

SUNDERLAND - where time is overtaking tradition

Bobby Gurney

IF Soccer has gone a little sour in Sunderland it is not just because the Roker Park club are no longer a power in the land and there are no more big names to captivate the hard-headed North Easterner.

The fact is that this once bustling seaport is on the decline. Times are hard just now in Durham; shipbuilding is not what it was, many of the pits are on the point of closing down and since the area admits to one of the highest current unemployment rates in the country the Wearsider has to look hard at the shillings in his pocket.

Relegated last season into the Second Division. Sunderland are having to make do with average home crowds of around 15,000 where once they came 40,000 strong to roar on "t' lads".

It costs 6s. on the terraces at Roker and while there is still money about a great deal of it is being spent in the clubs and pubs — especially the clubs, which have sprung up like mushrooms all over the Durham coalfield.

With a young and painfully inexperienced side (as I saw for myself), Sunderland are unlikely to get back into the First Division very quickly—not perhaps within the next three seasons. The club has no money now to buy the big stars on which they lavished huge fees in the immediate post-war years.

They live, too, in the shadow of Newcastle United, the ancient rivals who cut themselves a lucrative slice of Fairs Cup glory and have recaptured much of their glamour. And the loss of

those fiercely-fought derby games has knocked the heart out of the traditional inter-club ravalry, just when it was most needed to encourage Sunderland's supporters.

Six times First Division champions, F.A. Cup winners in 1937 with one of their best-ever sides in the modern era, Sunderland have had their fair share of success. Roker Park has known its great days—in 1933 it was jammed with 75,000 for a match against Derby—and the club once established a record by holding continuous membership of the First Division from 1890 to 1958.

Buchan, Thompson, Holley and Cuggy were the heroes of the pre-First World War period —a golden age in the club's history. During the regime of Johnny Cochrane, possibly Sunderland's most successful manager, from 1928 to 1939, fine players like Raich Carter, Johnny Mapson. Bobby Gurney, Eddie Burbanks, Fred Hall, Patsy Gallacher and Jimmy Connor delighted Roker fans with their skill and teamwork.

Since the last war, the procession of big names has been a long one—Trevor Ford. Len Shackleton, Willie Watson, Stan Anderson, Don Revie, Billy Bingham and Charlie Hurley, among others, have been the crowd pullers.

One of the greatest of all was Len Shackleton, for whom Sunderland paid neighbouring Newcastle the then considerable fee of £20,500, back in 1948. "Shack," prematurely white-haired, pipe-smoking and as shrewd as ever in his observa-

tions on the game, is still very much a name in the North East in his role as a Soccer columnist for a national Sunday newspaper.

He was at Roker Park the day I called. I found him gazing out over the pitch on which he enjoyed so many personal triumphs, the ground where his uncanny ball juggling was most appreciated.

"It's just not the same here. No crowds, no kids outside clamouring for autographs, no atmosphere in the town—it's a ghost ground to what it was," he said.

"They'll tell you here that all that is needed is patience . . . time to let the youngsters develop. But they've been saying that for too long. They have no money . . . there aren't the big names now, no glamour. It's a bit tragic."

One name I did see scrawled repeatedly on the walls of this so-called "ghost ground" within sound of the sad North Sea waves was "Toddo". This is Colin Todd, Sunderland's captain, an England Under-23 international mid-field player and once the youngest skipper in the First Division at 20.

Todd joined Sunderland straight from school at 15. He has been an outstanding performer in a struggling team over the past two seasons and at the time of writing his future at Roker was unsettled for he had asked for a transfer.

But he could well stay and Sunderland fans hope he will. A new team could be built around him and he is a great favourite with the younger supporters Sunderland are trying so hard to encourage.

Hope! There was more of it about than I first suspected when I got talking to some of the regular (and irregular) fans. In one club, I met supporters like *Nick Flaws* (30 years a regular), *Ernie Marwood*, now retired, who remembers watching Buchan and Holley and *John Reay*, a railwayman, who goes to Roker when shift work permits.

They agreed that the majority of Sunderland's loyal supporters want to see the club buy new players again, inject some glamour into the team. *"Aw mon, the gates would be up by 20 per cent,"* they told me.

Mr. Flaws admits that there

is some youthful talent in the current Sunderland team, but he would like to see an experienced centre-half like Charlie Hurley, who held the back line together for so many seasons. "*Too many gaps in the defence—especially when Toddo is out of the team,*" he claimed.

Mr. Reay recalled the old

Happier days . . . Charlie Hurley and Alan Brown after promotion had been clinched in 1964

SUNDERLAND–where time is overtaking tradition

days when the fans used to swarm across the Wear on the old ferry. *"We'd be there at 20 past two and still queueing at 10 past three. Those were the days when all Durham wanted to get into Roker,"* he said.

He, too, agreed that Sunderland needed more experience. Another Charlie Hurley was a *must*, he said. He had seen all the big stars at Roker, but thought there had been some bad buys and mismanagement in the past. "There's bags o' guts in t' team awt' same," he admitted. How long did he think it would take for Sunderland to get back?

"Aw, ah don't know, mon . . . but oor turn will coom."

Mr. Marwood, one of the real old school of supporters, has watched his team since he was 10 years old. He also thought Sunderland had wasted money on bad signings and this had led to their relegation.

"Jim Baxter was a poor investment," he pointed out. "So was Calvin Palmer." Baxter cost Sunderland £70,000 when they signed him from Rangers in 1965. In 1967, however, they sold him to Nottingham Forest for £100,000. Calvin Palmer cost £70,000 and that, all agreed, was one signing that "did not come off".

It seems, too, that last season, when Sunderland looked sure to go down, it was general knowledge in the town that a consor-

tium of local businessmen had offered to put £300,000 into the club—provided the old board resigned. They also planned to appoint former centre-forward Brian Clough as manager in place of Alan Brown.

It was said that at the time one prominent Sunderland director declared that given the choice of £300,000 and Brian Clough he would rather keep Alan Brown and do without the money!

Sunderland's confidence in Alan Brown is not too difficult to understand even in the club's present reduced circumstances. He is a man of rigid principles, of unbending dedication to duty, a man who has earned a reputation as being "hard"—a strict disciplinarian.

He is not to be trifled with—as many have discovered—but he has a warm and human side to his nature. He breeds tropical birds in what little spare time he has and calls his players "my children".

Now in his second spell with Sunderland, Brown has been a man of many parts. A post-war centre-half with Burnley, a former policeman and restaurateur, he has also seen service as a manager at Burnley and as a coach and manager with Sheffield Wednesday.

Brown *feels* for Sunderland, not just because he is a North Easterner but because he believes in the club and is just as

certain that they will rise again with their own home-grown team.

He denies that Sunderland are a "two-man team" . . . avers that there are other good players besides goalkeeper Jim Montgomery and Todd and Gordon Harris and Joe Baker.

Brown admits to a shortage of finance, but says, *"things here are not so black as some would have you believe."* The North East is still as prolific a nursery as ever it was.

Brown instanced five Sunderland youngsters who, he said, "are virtually unknown now, but will be household names in a few years." They are Mike McGiven (18), Richie Pitt (18), Bobby Park (18), Denis Tueart (20) and Billy Hughes (21). Tueart, Pitt and McGiven are North East boys, Park and Hughes from Coatbridge (Scotland). All have played First Division football—all have done well.

But the Sunderland manager's pride and joy is the new club training and recreational centre out at Washington, roughly midway between Wear and Tyne. And this could be the key to Sunderland's future.

Once, there was "nowt but the pit at Washington." Now there is a new town and big industrial developments are scheduled with the expectation that the population will top 100,000 in a few years' time. A huge new sports complex is planned and it is very possible that one day Sunderland may leave Roker and play at Washington. There has also been a suggestion that they might share a new super stadium with Newcastle United

for Washington, near the new motorway, is only about 15 minutes motoring distance from either club.

Already, there has been strenuous opposition to any ideas of Sunderland linking up with Newcastle. But for the moment Alan Brown is convinced that the Sunderland training headquarter will, in time, produce his new team and maybe a new era in the club's history.

Built on the same lines as Everton's Bellefield, this imposing centre boasts the largest indoor pitch in the country with dressing-rooms and baths attached, plus a recreational area where the players can relax.

It cost £112,000, raised largely from contributions and donations from supporters and others, and Brown started the fund off with £1,000 from his own pocket. He has also provided plants from his garden for the surrounding flower beds and most of his working day is spent there.

It is very much a long-term policy, but if Washington develops as planned there could be a whole new nursery of Soccer talent opened up. In recent years, too, many of the young men from the Durham mining villages have left the area for good as the pits have been worked out.

So Sunderland crowds may be in a depressed state as the club endures the painful experience of going through the inevitable transition period. But there is still hope and ambition for the future, even though time has overtaken tradition all too quickly for so many of the old Sunderland diehards.

Sunderland 1952-53: Back—F. Hall, W. Watson, H. Kirtley, J. Mapson, H. Threadgold, T. McNeil, W. Walsh, T. Reynolds, W. Bingham. Front: L. Shackleton, T. Wright, J. Hedley, T. Ford, J. Stelling, A. Wright, A. Hudgell.

**JIM
MONTGOMERY**
Sunderland

TODD HAS HAD TO FIGHT HIS WAY UP

Colin Todd in action (right). 'Sunderland have the potential to get back to the top'.

IT IS NOT hard to see how Sunderland skipper Colin Todd has become such a fine playing prospect. His unquestioned ability and level-headed approach to the game, plus his quiet, unassuming off-field manner, have endeared him to all at Roker Park.

It has turned out to be another bleak winter for 21-year-old Colin. A key-man in the Roker set-up, with England Under-23 caps behind him and full international honours beckoning, he has had to fashion his career with the Wearside club in a continuous struggle for stability.

For four seasons he has been caught up in a whirlpool of frustration that minimises his ambitions of winning League and Cup honours.

Towards the end of last season, Todd took on the added strain of captaincy, for what, by then, was clearly going to be a dog-fight to stay in the First Division.

Before he knew what had hit him, Todd had a man-sized job on his hands in a side entering a transitional period following the unloading of experienced campaigners like George Mulhall, George Herd, Ralph Brand and the old warhorse himself—Charlie Hurley.

A less equipped youngster might have folded under the pressure. But the extra responsibility, combined with his major role in the Sunderland back-four, helped him to develop even more quickly.

Despite overwhelming pressures, he has never once faltered in the cause of the club. He is a dedicated professional intent on helping to better the lot of success-starved supporters on Wearside.

But many fans are wondering how long he can be expected to bear the burden of Sunderland's struggles. And what effect the constant strain might have on his future career.

He has been almost an ever-present over the past three seasons—a fine tribute to his high-level consistency.

Todd joined Sunderland from school at 15 on the recommendation of chief scout Charlie Hughes, after rave reports of his displays for his Chester-Le-Street school and district sides and then Durham County Boys.

Many League clubs had taken a keen interest in him but Todd, born and bred in the North-East, plumped for Sunderland.

He was barely 17-years-old when he made his debut against Sheffield United at Bramall Lane in a League Cup-tie. Within six months he had won a regular place in the side.

Colin owes much of his playing progress to two people. Former favourite Charlie Hurley, who was always at hand to give advice, and Derby manager Brian Clough who groomed Sunderland's up-and-coming youngsters during his coaching days at Roker Park.

Pin him down to the match he most remembers and he picks Sunderland's F.A. Cup Fifth-round clash with Leeds in 1966-7. After two drawn games at Roker and Elland Road, the all-important decider ended in heated controversy at Boothferry Park, Hull, with Leeds getting a last-minute penalty win in extra-time, after two Sunderland players had been sent off.

After six years at Sunderland and despite the prolonged disappointments Colin Todd is optimistic about the future.

"We have some brilliant youngsters here," he says. "They have done really well, are eager to learn and go on improving. I'm convinced we have the talent and potential needed to get the club back to the top."

Who are these youngsters in whom manager Alan Brown and his skipper have placed their faith? They are: Dennis Tueart (20), an eager winger from Newcastle; Mick McGiven (19), also from Newcastle, and developing midfield man; Bobby Park (18) a Scot from Coatbridge and one of the most exciting prospects around; and the grafting Billy Hughes (21).

Says Todd: "It's a pity that things have been so difficult for them; they have come in at a bad time. It's tough when you are down at the bottom."

But that could be a blessing in disguise. Those youngsters have a good example of how to get by against the odds . . . COLIN TODD himself.

BOBBY
PARK
Sunderland

FOOTBALL
MONTHLY

Alan Brown's gamble on youth

Sunderland can stay up there with the top six

by David Wright

JOHN LATHAN . . . youngster who is grabbing goals

SUNDERLAND'S topsy-turvy form is one of Soccer's newest mysteries.

It's been stop-go-stop for the Roker men, who have been trapped in a grip of inconsistency that has dragged them into the lower half of the Second Division table.

After losing the opening game to North East rivals Middlesbrough, Sunderland settled into a promising run of seven games without defeat and talk of promotion, which they had narrowly missed out on last season, began to occupy the thoughts of the Roker fans.

An upset at Villa Park was followed by a resounding home win over relegated Nottingham Forest, but then they hit trouble—with an almighty thud.

They were hammered by a Hugh Curran-inspired Oxford to the tune of 5-1 despite leading at half-time. A week later Sunderland suffered their first home defeat of the season when Luton beat them 2-0, and then they lost 2-3 to Q.P.R.

So one of manager Alan Brown's greatest concerns in the last couple of weeks has been to try and restore confidence to his young side.

Brown will have been assuring them that there is a long way to go and they are capable of making up the lost ground.

To do this, however, Sunderland can't afford to drop many home points, and so it's vitally important to them that they beat Aston Villa at Roker on Saturday.

As Villa's slip has also been showing recently—only one point from the games with Fulham, Queen's Park Rangers and Blackpool—Sunderland must rate their chances of gaining revenge for their defeat in the Midlands nearly six weeks ago.

In spite of losing by two goals, the Wearsiders left a very favourable impression at Aston Villa. Indeed, Villa skipper Bruce Rioch commented afterwards that Sunderland were the best side they had faced so far.

Sunderland took the initiative from the start and applied heavy pressure on Villa's defence, but they were unable to translate their superiority into goals.

"We were relieved when Alun Evans put us ahead and when I scored from a 25 yard free-kick," said Rioch.

The Villa skipper said he was staggered that Sunderland gave him a clear shot at goal. "They didn't even put a wall up. It was like giving me a penalty from 25 yards.

"I hope I get a few more chances like that." Rioch can be sure that Sunderland won't make any similar errors on Saturday.

The fact that Sunderland have been making errors, and consequently dropping points, could be blamed on their lack of experience. For they have one of the youngest sides in the Football League.

Manager Brown is gambling heavily on youth this season, youngsters like their top goal grabber John Lathan, though some Roker fans have been saying that he is pitching too many boys into a man's game.

Brown would hardly agree, of course. And as 21-year-old defender Ritchie Pitt says: "If the boss doesn't play them how else can they get experience?

"All young players are raw and that's probably why the boss is playing them, to gain this vital experience."

Sunderland-born Pitt, who took over the No. 5 shirt from Eire international Charlie Hurley, won back his place two weeks ago after a spell in the reserves and is now determined to keep a first-team spot.

Despite Sunderland's oscillating form, Pitt still believes they will finish in the top six.

"We've got the players capable of making us a better side than last season, when we just failed to get promoted. But whether we are a better footballing side is not easy to say."

There will be few harder tests of their ability than the clash with Villa this weekend.

...and a brilliant selection of styles

FOOTBALL MONTHLY

RITCHIE PITT
Sunderland

DAVID WATSON Sunderland

BOBBY KERR

'I'M ENJOYING MY NEW ROVING MISSION'

AN EARLY season switch of positions, caused by injuries two weeks in succession, led to a remarkable transformation in the form of Sunderland forward Bobby Kerr.

Young Kerr, the lad who suffered two broken legs which forced him to miss almost two years football a couple of seasons back, started out this season in his usual position on the wing.

But then, in Sunderland's first match of the season at Roker Park, Bobby Park broke his leg early on in the game. John Porterfield moved out of midfield to fill the vacant full-back spot and Kerr moved inside. And the next week, when Sunderland suffered another injury, Kerr again moved inside.

CONVERTED

He said: "I seemed to do a lot more in the middle than on the wing and the manager noticed this. So I stayed in midfield for the next few matches and I began to enjoy it a lot. Now I'm a converted player.

"I've been playing in the middle of the park with a sort of roving mission—helping in attacks and then picking up and marking someone in defence—and I have been happy with my play so far this season.

"I was out on the wing all last season—my first full season in the senior side—but in some games I was using a lot of energy and in others, I was just going through a game. That was no good to me.

"Now, I can go where I like —I'm not restricted.

CENTURY

"And I seem to have the energy to keep going in attack and, if I'm put on a man, I can pick him up and stick to him.

"I enjoy this sort of roving game and, although I don't think I am scoring as many goals as I did last season, I think the lads are sharing them out more now.

"A few have got almost the same total and others are not

far behind, whereas last season there were a couple with 10 and the next highest would only have about four."

Kerr joined Sunderland straight from school and recently made his 100th appearance for the Roker Park side. Apart from the very experienced players in the side—like full-back Martin Harvey who has made over 300 appearances, goalkeeper Jim Montgomery (more than 350), full-back Cecil

BOBBY KERR
Sunderland

Irwin (approaching 350) and ex-Burnley schemer Gordon Harris (nearly 150 for Sunderland)—Kerr, although still only 24, is one of the established players in a mainly young side.

And, as Kerr says, Sunderland are now beginning to reap the benefits from several years of success at youth team level.

"In the last four to five years we have always had a good youth side and have been there or thereabouts in most junior

competitions," he said.

"We are now just beginning to get the benefits of the young lads. One of the biggest advantages of having a young side is that, even if you're getting beaten, you know you will still get 100 per cent effort from them whereas if you have a lot of older players, they tend to throw in the sponge.

FEARS

"Although we are basically a young side, we have a fair amount of experience in the club, for, even our young lads have been in the game too long to be made to look like novices.

"A lot of the youngsters got experience in the year we were relegated from the First Division and I think we have got rid of any fears we might have had of that division. We had fears when we were in it and that was half the trouble—we always felt lower than the other team. But now we feel on top of the world.

"I think we've got the same sort of set-up now as Derby had when they were promoted —we have the skill and certainly a lot of young players. I think a lot of managers have got a high regard for Sunderland these days even when we are away from home. And at Roker Park, teams have had nine men in defence and that's something which has never happened before."

TASTE

Kerr believes the present side is good enough to gain promotion—if not this season, certainly next or the one after. And, as he says, with most of the younger players already having had a taste of life in the top division, Sunderland may have a better base on which to build a successful First Division set-up in the years to come.

So maybe Kerr's hopes "for crowds of 40,000 at Roker" will yet be fulfilled—and Sunderland may begin to rival some of the great teams which the club produced in years gone by.

BOB STOKOE
—the man who has to work a miracle

SUNDERLAND'S SAVIOUR

By ERIC NICHOLLS

BOB STOKOE eased himself into the manager's chair at Roker Park and his face creased into the kind of smile that said it all. Bob was home. Among his own people and among friends.

"Look," he says, "we Geordies are a clannish lot. That's why this job is a bit special. I wouldn't have left Blackpool for any club. But to manage one of the big clubs here is every Geordie's dream. When the opportunity came I just had to jump at it.

"To me, it's the fulfilment of a lifetime's ambition in sight. And I have the opportunity I feel I have worked hard for.

"When Sunderland came for me, I was thrilled. I wasn't exactly over the moon. I've been in this game long enough to keep my feet on the ground. But it gave me a lift, a feeling of tremendous pride.

"You see, it's not just a question of coming home. I feel I've earned the right to come home. I went away to learn my trade. You don't get a manager's job with a big club when you have finished playing. Joe Harvey went to Barrow and Workington before taking over at Newcastle.

"I went South for the experience. I was a foreigner among foreigners. But it didn't make any difference. I was there to learn and picking up what I could from people like Bill Nicholson and Dave Sexton made it all worthwhile."

The 42-year-old Stokoe is the man Sunderland see as their salvation. And that's not to put too fine a point on a situation that finds Sunderland puffing hard for points at the wrong end of the Second Division.

And what he calls his going-away-to-learn period is good enough reason for Sunderland to look to him. Bury were nearly promoted in his first season with them, Rochdale were kept in the Fourth Division—they are now in the Third—at a time when to apply for re-election might have killed them off.

Charlton were saved from relegation, Carlisle consolidated and Blackpool, near-misses for promotion, reached two Anglo-Italian finals and took the trophy once.

Charlton sacked him in what Stokoe describes as the only blot on a career that has spanned 25 years, but in every managerial post the straight-talking Geordie was making his mark and setting his course for home.

They couldn't have picked a more dedicated man. For Stokoe will not rest until Sunderland are back in the First Division.

He says: "When you look at how well Norwich and Ipswich are doing you know Sunderland should be in the First. So should Middlesbrough.

"I know Stan Anderson has been working with this aim at Middlesbrough and we all know we have a much better football area than East Anglia. I'm sure Stan will agree when I say we won't rest until Tyneside, Wearside and Teesside are together again in the First Division.

"There used to be a tremendous rivalry between Newcastle and Sunderland. There isn't today, simply because we aren't in the First Division."

Talking of the First Division while his club are struggling to avoid relegation may sound as though Stokoe has got his priorities wrong.

But he says: "The First has got to be our aim. Keeping ourselves in the Second is only the short-term fight. It's unthinkable that this club should drop into the Third."

Sunderland have become renowned over the past few seasons for their emphasis on youth. And for all the high promise and obvious ability of young players like Joe Latham, Mike Horswill and Jack Ashurst, it is one of the game's most common philosophies that experience is better than promise when you are in trouble.

Says Stokoe: "This is something I've been looking at over the past couple of weeks. We have a long way to go yet, but things have got to be sorted out quickly. I've given the lads their head and it has been up to them to prove what they can do.

"But the balance of the side is important and I've got to consider who I could buy to tip the scales in our favour. But I'm not interested in short-term buys."

Stokoe believes that the club's position does not reflect the talent at Roker. He says: "I'm always an optimist, but I honestly believe our position is a little bit false. We can't kid ourselves and we must be aware how close the Third Division is.

"We have a young staff and a couple of extra men would give us the time to bring the youngsters along. Certainly, we have the facilities here to develop a youth policy, and this has already been proved.

"If I can get the same level of consistency and ability I got at Carlisle and Blackpool, we have the basic talent to go places."

Bob Stokoe has achieved one goal by making it back to the North-East. Now he knows he has to make that journey worthwhile.

NEXT WEEK: I waited five years for revenge

STOKOE the proud skipper of Newcastle. The year: 1956. The team: back row, left to right: Keery, Taylor, Keith, Simpson, Batty, Crowe: front row: Davies, Keeble, Stokoe, Hannah and Mitchell. The position: centre-half. And in 1956 centre-halves didn't come much bigger—or much better

We won't give City stars any room to shine

by David Wright

says IAN PORTERFIELD

FRANCIS LEE . . . will take an awful lot of stopping

STAR-STUDDED Manchester City, lingering for so long in the shadow of that other crowd from across town, can blaze their way back into the limelight on Saturday by taking another step along the F.A. Cup glory trail.

The Cup offers this Soccer crazy Northern city its sole remaining opportunity of getting among the honours this season, and Malcolm Allison's men have never been more determined to bring the trophy to Maine Road.

Sunderland, however, are barring their route and they, too, have more than a burning desire to win through to the last eight. But City present Sunderland with their greatest test since manager Bob Stokoe inspired a revival in the Second Division club's fortunes.

The new spirit of rejuvenated Sunderland is reflected in midfield man Ian Porterfield's comment: "We are prepared to go out on to the park and die for the club."

This, says 27-year-old Porterfield, is the attitude that Bob Stokoe has injected into his players since his arrival nearly three months ago.

"The boss is a bad loser and this has rubbed off on to us," adds Scot Porterfield. "He has really shaken the club up, the players' spirits have been lifted, and the fans are coming back."

Stokoe has done a remarkable job in such a short time. He has lifted Sunderland off the floor and instilled so much confidence into the players that they confront Manchester City with more than a hope of victory.

City have world-class players in Francis Lee, Rodney Marsh and Colin Bell, but, as was emphatically proved in the Fourth Round, the mighty can be toppled as easily as the minnows.

"The way we're playing these days, we must be in with a good chance of getting a result," says Porterfield, a key figure in Sunderland's midfield department who is nearing his 150th League appearance for the club.

"It's going to be hard, very hard. We know that. City have a lot of exceptionally good players. But we can play them tight, stop them from turning and getting into their stride, then we'll be there with a chance.

"A lot, I think, depends on the early stages. If we can soak their early pressure we'll become more confident and then perhaps we'll be able to start pushing up a bit. There's a lot of experience in our side. We're not giving many goals away and we're knocking in a few ourselves.

"We have a great deal of respect for for-

PORTERFIELD . . . prepared to die for Sunderland

wards like Rodney Marsh, Francis Lee and Mike Summerbee. They're all internationals and players who've got to be feared. If you give them room you're asking for trouble. Our defence has got to be on its toes and stay right on top of them."

Criticisms of the Sunderland defence were made after their Fourth Round tie with Fourth Division Reading. "They look very vulnerable under pressure," said one of the Reading players.

And Reading manager Charlie Hurley, who wore Sunderland's No. 5 shirt with such distinction for 12 years, shares this view, saying: "Midfield and up front they're a good side. But defensively I think they could struggle against a side like Manchester City. Lee, Bell and Summerbee will run hard at them and will take an awful lot of stopping."

Sunderland say they have a man capable of stemming the inevitable flow of City attacks—and that's big Dave Watson. This solidly-built player, who bears a striking resemblance to Tony Hateley, is one of the country's most versatile performers.

Watson, who has scored three of the six goals that his team have scored in the Cup this season, can operate in defence or attack with equal efficiency. But it's virtually certain that he'll be wearing the No. 5 shirt at Maine Road, allowing Vic Halom, Sunderland's recent £35,000 signing from Luton, into the attack.

"They can't play him anywhere else," is Charlie Hurley's expert opinion. "Watson is not overloaded with skill, but he's very good in the air and a hard tackler."

Says Porterfield: "We can rely on Dave to get 90 to 95 per cent of the balls in the air and this gives the rest of the lads confidence. He's got tremendous heading ability. And we'll certainly need him against City for Mike Summerbee is such a brilliant crosser of the ball."

Sunderland's visit on Saturday is a good omen for Manchester City. They have met the Roker men on four previous occasions in the F.A. Cup and twice gone on to reach the final—in 1904, when they beat Bolton, and again in 1955, when City lost to Newcastle. Will it be City's turn again this season? Not until Sunderland have had their say.

A teenage terrier in midfield, that's Mike Horswill who played such a big part in Sunderland's great rally in the season's second half

SUNDERLAND

Watson could cause a shock

DAVE WATSON

by ERIC NICHOLLS

DAVE WATSON, a one-man success story in his own right during the Sunderland revival, steps out against the might of Arsenal on Saturday to prove that he—and his side—are worth a place in the F.A. Cup final.

In a game that manager Bob Stokoe has described as "just the one I fancied" Watson must face two of the finest strikers in the game in John Radford or Charlie George and Ray Kennedy.

But that won't deter dynamic Dave. He knows all about the striking part. He was one for Sunderland for some time and his switch to the back has been one of the happiest success stories in Soccer.

Dave scored Sunderland's first goal against Luton in the quarter-final—a diving header from a corner. But it is as a defender that he earns this high praise from Stokoe: "He's international class. He proved it against Manchester City and he proved it again against Luton. That's if it needed proving.

"I look at him and I realise he is like a steeple among defenders. I saw him as a platform on which to build the defence when I came here and that's why I decided the switching from centre-half to centre-forward had to stop."

Stokoe's wisdom and Watson's insistence that "I prefer the centre-half position" has combined to give Sunderland the kind of stability at the back they are going to need more than ever on Saturday.

But it will also serve as a guideline to Sunderland's progress towards their main aim—a return to First Division status.

Arsenal and Sunderland have clashed three times in the F.A. Cup. Sunderland winning twice—once by 6-0—and Arsenal gaining the other victory.

Now that they are 90 minutes away from Wembley, Stokoe's men will not be any kind of pushover on Saturday, despite their current Second Division status.

But what of Watson, the man now chased by a nation-wide posse of scouts, but practically unheard of outside Wearside a year ago?

He admits to owing his success to four people and one club. Brother Tony, Tommy Docherty, Alan Brown and David Coates are the men, Notts County the club.

Alan Brown signed him from Rotherham. Rotherham boss Tommy Docherty had bought him from Notts County and brother Tony gave him his ambitious spark.

Says Dave: "My brother kept at me to push myself after I had played a couple of games for Nottingham schools. Some of the lads were rushing all over the place for trials, but not me. But from Tony's experience as a non-league manager he knew I had it in me. He told me to have a go, so I wrote to County for a trial."

David Coates was coach at County and after the club had taken Dave on, he nursed him through those early days when Watson turned out in nine different positions.

Rotherham was a step up and Dave says: "I'll always be grateful to Tommy Docherty for taking me there."

But as the Doc says: "He was a natural. He'd got so many talents and in the air he could get up so high and stay up there so long that you felt you had to get the loud hailer out and shout, 'Come in number 5, you're time's up'. Add to that the fact that he's a great fellow and a players' professional and you've just about said it all."

The Doc moved on from Rotherham, but didn't forget Watson. His name cropped up in almost every football conversation and eventually Alan Brown moved in to take him to the North-East.

Brown, like coaches before him, spotted the versatility of Watson, but his switches at Roker were confined to the no. 5 and no. 10 jerseys.

That was until Stokoe took over and made one of the most important decisions of his managerial career.

Dave goes along with the idea and results have shown both to be right. And this is

VIC HALOM . . . ace goal-grabber of the Roker side

one of Stokoe's most important keys in the battle to return to the First Division.

Certainly Dave agrees on that one. He says: "International appearances and Cup runs are bonuses for a footballer. They're great and obviously I'd like to be considered for the England squad.

"But my main objective and that of the rest of the lads here is First Division football with Sunderland. And the way we are playing at the moment, and with the spirit we have here, I can see that coming before very long."

Nobody would argue with that sentiment. But there's every chance that there are F.A. Cup shocks to come before that.

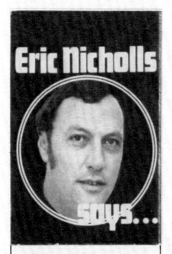

Eric Nicholls says...

INSTANT DISCIPLINE in the form of a Soccer sin-bin is likely to be a surprise item on the agenda for the Football League chairmen at their annual meeting in June.

The League Management Committee have been quietly canvassing opinion and quite a few clubs are in favour of an experimental period for dishing out short-term punishment for minor offences.

The idea is not new. It has been banded about for more than a decade and would mean players spending short periods—say five minutes—off the field instead of being booked and collecting penalty points.

I believe the reformers are both right and wrong. Right to feel anger at the almost comic state of affairs where clubs lodge appeals as a matter of course to ensure players are available for important matches.

Wrong to mess about with the basics of the game.

The disciplinary machine is being taken for a ride by people who have clearly put their own interests before the interests of the game.

But I'm inclined to go along with Liverpool's Bill Shankly who doesn't believe the game should be interfered with to such an extent.

Shankly feels the problem is best left to the managers, players and referees.

He is right. Because the public would never stand for a "stunt" that is foreign to the game.

And because such a scheme would pose so many problems, a sin-bin would either become a farce—or prove unworkable.

The fans would never tolerate a game with players going off and on like a basketball "time-out".

And this is how it could end up unless there was a restriction on the number of players from each team in the sin-bin at any one time.

That again could defeat the object of the exercise.

No, the professionals who make or break the game must have the courage to put their own house in order.

THE NIGHT SUNDERLAND WENT MAD

NOT FOR more than 30 years has Sunderland known anything like it. Not since 1937 has the town's football team provoked such scenes of wild joy as they did last Saturday after that defeat of Arsenal which put Sunderland into the F.A. Cup final.

Not since the immortal Raich Carter and the rest of the triumphant Cup-winning side returned home after beating Preston 3-1 in Sunderland's last Wembley appearance have Sunderland folk had such an excuse for running the town almost dry of that famous brown ale, the Geordies' own brew.

Ironically, Preston were the last Second Division side to get to Wembley, where they lost 3-2 to West Ham in 1964.

But the prospect of following Preston in defeat, even against mighty Leeds, could not have been in the minds of those joyful fans, who returned home from Hillsborough to join the unfortunate ones who had been unable to get tickets. They united in crazy dances in the streets and singing in the pubs until well after closing time.

And as they celebrated, one man's name was on everyone's lips. That name was Bob Stokoe, who was the toast of every happy Roker fan.

For it was Stokoe, a true Geordie himself, a commanding member of the Newcastle defence in their side which brought back the Cup after beating Manchester City 18 years ago, who has transformed Sunderland from a modest, uninspired outfit into a side capable of beating the best with the most inspired football.

Whatever Sunderland achieve against Leeds, the side they were last promoted with to the First Division in 1964, Stokoe will be known as the man who led Sunderland from the wilderness.

The goals that took them to Wembley

VIC HALOM (centre) knows it. So, too, does Arsenal goalkeeper Bob Wilson. It's a goal and Sunderland are on their way to Wembley and a day of glory

WILSON IS beaten again, this time by Billy Hughes (second left) and it's all over for Arsenal— or very nearly. Charlie George's late goal was not enough

TAMING ARSENAL

Nobody played a bigger part in sending Sunderland on the glory trail to Wembley than keeper Jim Montgomery seen (above) making a great semi-final save, watched by Ray Kennedy, Ritchie Pitt, Dave Watson, Jeff Blockley and Ron Guthrie. (Below) Roker men Dick Malone, Mickey Horswill and Ian Porterfield watch George Armstrong attack

That old Wembley feeling

No wonder Billy Hughes and Mike Horswill look pleased . . . they're celebrating Sunderland's winning goal against Arsenal in the semi-final

THE FOOTBALL WRITER READ BY MILLIONS

Thanks, Bob Stokoe, now we can all believe again

The men who make Sunderland tick . . . the men who have exploded the Roker Park side to Wembley glory: trainer Billy Elliott, Tyrolean-hatted Stokoe and, extreme right, coach Arthur Cox

BOB STOKOE should not be embarrassed when he recalls the tears shed in the delirious echo of an F.A. Cup semi-final triumph. For the Sunderland manager, it was a joyous moment. For us all, it was an opportunity to appreciate what the game is all about.

Some six months ago Sunderland were being offered as a critical example of mismanagement, a club seemingly threatened with bankruptcy and certainly burdened with debt.

Once powerful, and with a colourful history of massive transfer outlay, they had drifted into comparative anonymity. The corniest of jokes applied.

"What time does the game start?"
"What time can you get here?"

It all changed with the coming of Stokoe, a man with his heart in the north-east and with a talent for revival. Sunderland will go to Wembley for the F.A. Cup final and football should be grateful for the achievement.

Even allowing for the peculiar nature of the circumstances and the well of enthusiasm still there to be tapped, Stokoe has helped to recharge a popularity not only of Sunderland but of football itself.

Success of course is all-important. And the F.A. Cup is invested with magical properties.

But what Stokoe has unashamedly shown is that football need not bury itself in a mood of excessive organisation. Its strategy may be harder to understand and speed has certainly suffocated the more extravagant forms of individuality. But what should not be overlooked is that, if the circumstances are right, the passion is still there.

Sunderland's progress over the past few months has been in every way romantic, encouraging others to recognise the value of contesting what may seem to be a lost cause.

It was right that Bob Stokoe should shed tears in a moment of overwhelming joy. It was a natural emotion, surprising perhaps for people who have never dug beneath the more forbidding veneer of his Geordie background.

Victory uncovered a sensitive man. A man who hates losing but who is willing to share his successes with the world.

There are those who will see this as a betrayal of what sport should mean to its competitors. The outmoded gospel of losing well and taking defeat lightly. But let other sports invest in stiff upper-lipped images. Football can do without one.

Stokoe may find it all a bit unreal. Four years ago he was sacked by Charlton and remembers that as the most demoralising moment of his career. He believed that he was doing the right thing, basically the same things which he has applied at Roker Park. Experience may indeed have sharpened his technique, but his principles are those which were there the day Charlton lost at Crystal Palace . . . the day Stokoe was told he wasn't wanted any more.

He had the courage to begin again at the bottom. To work towards what he felt was his rightful place in the business. Rochdale first, Carlisle, and then Blackpool, recognised his quality. Sunderland, although showing a keenness for someone with a more established reputation, were finally convinced by his style. In turn, Stokoe has proved that he is more

than adequately equipped for the job.

Football has been reborn at Roker where it is no longer necessary to yearn for days gone by and the names who helped make them memorable.

Sunderland, for all their romantic significance, remain in the Second Division, and promotion will be the dominant feature in Stokoe's thinking. But it is now possible to believe in what might have seemed a wild and unsupported dream.

It should be enough to recognise that football needed what Sunderland have achieved this season. Had they drifted even deeper into depression there would have been every reason to suppose that bankruptcy was a very real prospect for at least a third of the League's clubs.

The best of them will be encouraged. The worst of them can at least take heart.

And for managers whose only reward is a dismal, admonishing lack of gratitude on the part of their directors, Stokoe's enthusiasm and durability will be important.

It hasn't been easy for him. He's known his bad times and he may know them again. The important thing is that he had good cause to stand out there and lose himself in joy.

KERR...
The flyweight who feels 10 feet tall

by RAY
BRADLEY

FORMER Sunderland manager Alan Brown once described him as "a mini with a Rolls-Royce engine". Current supremo Bob Stokoe affectionately refers to him as "my little general".

Two vividly descriptive views from past and present that clearly underline the Tartan talents of Bobby Kerr, Sunderland's mighty midget and inspiring skipper.

Although mini maestro Kerr stands only 5 ft. 4½ in. high (a full inch shorter than rival skipper Billy Bremner) and weighs in at 9 st. 4 lb., he has clearly proved you don't have to be a giant to succeed in a very physical game.

Bobby's lack of inches is a standing joke in the dressing-room and he's always the first to crack: "When they see me leading out the team they think I'm the mascot." But he has no hang-ups about his natural disadvantages.

Characteristically he claims in a soft Scots brogue that is slightly tinged with adopted Geordie: "Look man, when I lead out Sunderland I feel 10 feet tall. Size doesn't matter in this game: it's how big your heart is that counts.

"I feel pride and passion because I'm the boss man on the field. I'm captain of Sunderland and that really means something up here where the fans live and die for football."

The sort of burning pride and courage that helped Bobby to bounce back from two broken legs in a 10-year pro career at Roker.

Ironically, the first break came six years ago in a fifth round Cup battle with Saturday's Wembley opponents Leeds.

"It was just a clash of shins with Norman Hunter," says Bobby coolly and without animosity. "It was a pure accident and there's no mental scars likely to be stirred up on Saturday.

"The second break was really the bigger shock. It came in my third comeback game for the reserves and I didn't realise the right leg was broken again until the X-ray revealed it.

"Both breaks impressed upon me the stupidity of not wearing shin pads. I'm wiser now. I've learned my lesson the hard way and I won't go on the park without them ever again."

Sunderland's midfield general is a player who rhymes skill with will and has been a model of consistency over the last few seasons and a courageous competitor in the Bremner mould despite his size.

His bubbling enthusiasm on the field (he takes most throw-ins and corner kicks) was rewarded last season when he took over from Martin Harvey as skipper of the side.

Although he was ideally suited for such promotion, both temperamentally and because of his natural enthusiasm, Bobby admits: "I used to find it a bit of a chore at first. I used to bottle things up and take them home with me.

"I suppose I got too involved on the responsibility side. I used to get really worked up after a game analysing my own contribution too much. Now I find I can forget about these things and I'm beginning to enjoy the responsibility."

His attitude to the job is clearly spelt

BOBBY KERR . . . He came back after two broken legs

out when he admits: "It's taken time to fully adjust to the role. Frank McLintock leads by his personality and drive. He's a dominant captain with lots of experience at the job.

"I prefer to think I lead by example. I feel I've got to go full out for 90 minutes every game. There's no resting periods in any case in midfield. But I've been given a job to do and I give it all I've got.

"But my job is made a lot easier at Sunderland because we're all going full out. There are no slackers in the side and that makes my job easier."

Of his own particular midfield job he says: "I'm basically a striker and personally feel that I can play a lot better. But our front three are playing so brilliantly at the moment that Ian Porterfield and I have to play more defensively.

"We are not so attack-conscious now because we can't afford to leave gaps. I'm working more in the middle but I still prefer to go up and support attacks.

"This is my tenth year with the club and it's obviously been our most successful season. It's been a hard slog to achieve success and we're even more delighted for our fans. But the big test will come next season. We've set a terrific standard in the last four months. We will have to live up to it next season."

And Leeds? "They are a team I admire tremendously," adds Bobby. "But they are only 11 men, not 11 supermen. We've beaten Manchester City and Arsenal on merit. We've got to Wembley on merit. That's the great thing that inspires confidence.

"If Leeds underestimate us they'll be in for a shock. They may have 11 internationals, but we've got more workers. We've sweated to get to Wembley and there'll be no easing up now."

ROADS TO
SUNDERLAND

THIRD ROUND
    Notts Co. 1-1 (Watson)
    Notts Co. 2-0 (Watson, Tueart)
FOURTH ROUND
    Reading 1-1 (Tueart)
    Reading 3-1 (Watson, Tueart, Kerr)
FIFTH ROUND
    Man. City 2-2 (Horswill, Hughes)
    Man. City 3-1 (Halom, Hughes 2)
SIXTH ROUND:
    Luton 2-0 (Watson, Guthrie)
SEMI-FINAL:
    Arsenal 2-1 (Halom, Hughes)

Sunderland's glorious Cup victory... and now a magical cash triumph, says ALAN HUGHES

BOB STOKOE – THE ONE-YEAR MILLIONAIRE

THE MAGICIAN to whom the gods gave the down-to-earth name of Bob Stokoe has now opened the door to one of the most astonishing financial feats of all Soccer time.

Come early December, when he will celebrate—if that isn't an understatement—his first twelve months as manager of Sunderland, the Roker Park club aim to be raking in the MILLIONTH quid since Stokoe arrived, with nothing but faith in himself to meet a bunch of players who had lost all faith in themselves.

YES, ONE MILLION POUNDS. And this is the way they'll do it . . .

From Roker gates since Stokoe's arrival, they've already taken in the region of £250,000.

From the F.A. Cup Final and the semi-final at Hillsborough, they've hauled in more than £75,000.

From season tickets for the 1973-74 promotion-pushing season they are reckoning on another quarter of a million when they can get round to tackling the avalanche of applications.

From even a modest run in the European Cup Winners' Cup they can expect around £35,000 each time they play at capacity packed Roker Park.

And from around ten League games at Roker between the start of the season and the beginning of December they can expect something in the region of £20,000 a match from the turnstiles to augment the season ticket sales.

That comes to about £850,000, and programmes, and other ancillaries will boost the figure to the magic million.

Not bad for a club whose home gates before Stokoe's arrival were down to 12,000-odd, at a time when most of Sunderland's disillusioned Soccer citizens were reckoning that you had to be odd if you were still going to Roker.

But it is a reward that the most popular F.A. Cup-winners of all time deeply deserve.

As Stokoe himself said of that unforgettable Wembley triumph. "We played them the way we said we would and we beat them the way we said we would, at football."

And Dave Watson, the people's choice as the Man of the Match said: "Leeds expected to have room to play First Division style football and we didn't give them any.

"Quite honestly they weren't as good as I expected them to be."

BOB STOKOE hoisted aloft in his moment of glory, and (below) the traditional pose of Cup winners, with Bobby Kerr proudly showing the Cup

THAT'S IT. The goal that took the Cup to Wearside. Sunderland whoop for joy as Ian Porterfield's shot nestles in the Leeds net. But it took two incredible saves from Jim Montgomery—seen below punching clear from Mick Jones—to assure victory. Another hero was Dave Watson, who completely overshadowed Allan Clarke (below right)

Jim Montgomery's 'save of the century'

Bob Stokoe: A manager is only as good as his players and I give all my thanks and praise to my players. The final didn't frighten us. I told the lads to go out there and give us a great final. At half-time I told them to go out and give us a great victory. This win has come at the end of a wonderful five months with these lads. I'm proud of them all. But our keeper, Jimmy Montgomery, was my man of the match for making those two marvellous saves. His save from Peter Lorimer was one of the most incredible I have ever seen.

Jimmy Montgomery: I'm not sure if it was the best save I've ever made, but it was certainly the most important. I just threw myself into the air, but I didn't know the ball hadn't gone into the net until our fans roared.

Ritchie Pitt: A fantastic save. I don't know how Monty got to it.

Peter Lorimer: I had all the time I wanted, and all the goal to shoot at. When I swung my foot the keeper was at the far side of the goal. Don't ask me how he got to it.

Johnny Giles: That save was the turning point. If it had gone in, we would have won.

Billy Bremner: Sunderland played very well, although we had them going in the second half. They got the break at the right time. We're used to disappointments, and we'll be back.

Don Revie: They deserved to win it without any shadow of doubt. They played particularly well in the first half. They were quick into the tackle and never allowed us to settle. We sat back in the first half and gave them an awful amount of room. But we pushed more up in the second half. We have no excuses. Now we have to get on our feet and start working again for the Cup Winners' Cup Final in Greece.

Ian Porterfield: It's absolutely fantastic to score the winning goal. Wembley suited my style.

Oh, Mr, Porterfield, whatever did you do... You went and sc

HA'WAY THE LAI

THE DRAMA is over. The accolades have ceased. But for some of us—yes, many outside Roker Park too—the memory will live on. Of Second Division Sunderland stepping out at Wembley to crunch mighty Leeds . . . of red track-suited Bob Stokoe doing his own bit on that famous turf . . . and of Ian Porterfield slamming the goal that mattered with his "wrong" foot. These and many more memories will live with us for a long time yet. So we're proud to be able to help you to compile those very special scrapbooks to show the kids when they get older. Perhaps, for Sunderland people, even the grandchildren. So here's a spread of colour pictures to make the day complete. They tell the story far better than any words of ours could do.

MICK JONES and RON GUTHRIE run side by side, but with opposite causes to fight for

THE THREE MUSKETEERS . . . Sunderland's DENNIS TUEART, IAN PORTERFIELD and RITCHIE PITT in the line-up

...l at Wembley and made all Bob Stokoe's dreams come true

S...Sun-der-land...!

IT'S all over and even the uninitiated know who's won. The colours, the Cup, and the smiles all belong to Sunderland

HALOM IS AMBITIOUS FOR THE BIG-TIME

by Eric Nicholls

VIC HALOM . . . showing the dash and skill that makes him so valuable to Sunderland

VIC HALOM has been to Wembley to acknowledge the cheers and has experienced a kind of star treatment he always believed was reserved for others.

But he is my transfer bargain of the season because he supplied the vital link to set Sunderland's attack Wembley bound.

Previously they had produced plenty of skill and goal potential. But they lacked height and power. Halom has given them that and at £30,000 he must qualify for his bargain buy tag in one of the shortest possible times.

Halom only joined his old boss Bob Stokoe in February and says: "It was only Bob and Sunderland that made me accept their offer. I wasn't unhappy at Luton or anything like that. But I have such tremendous respect for Bob.

"After all, it was he who brought me into football as a lad with Charlton. I'll always remember when Bob got the sack. I was recovering from a cartilage operation and Bob sent me on loan to Orient because Dick Graham had just taken them over and Bob felt he was just the right sort of hard man to help me back to fitness.

"I couldn't believe it when I heard the news and even though I was still their player, I had no heart for Charlton after that."

But Bob Stokoe never forgot and says now: "It wasn't a question of getting rave reports about Vic. But I knew he could do a job for us and every player has to settle down sometime. I felt he could do it with us."

He certainly has, and admits his own ambitions when he says: "I'm still only 24, and for the first time I feel I have the opportunity to make it to the big time."

While Halom looks to a bright footballing future in the North-East, his thriving electrical contracting business in Luton offers security for himself and his family.

As he says: "The business was going fine. It was good for me to get away from football and think about other things and be clear to concentrate on match days.

"Everything in our set-up was fine, including a nice house. We were happy. Then Bob came along . . ."

VIC HALOM . . . sharing in the Sunderland glory parade at Wembley

BRITAIN'S CUP KINGS

Few people outside of Wearside gave Sunderland a chance of beating Leeds. Most critics thought Celtic would complete the Double by beating Rangers. But the marvellous uncertainty of football was never better illustrated as Sunderland and Rangers became Cup Kings of Britain - in great style, too.

THE CUP STORY WHICH

Bob Stokoe

MIRACLE-MAN OF ROKER

WELL, how else would we *dare* open this book other than with Sunderland and Stokoe and the greatest giant-killing story since Ipswich Town won the Football League Championship in 1961-62?

Greater in fact . . .

For while the Town, unfashionable and unfancied, still competed on level terms with their 21 First Division rivals, Stokoe's red-and-whites set out on their Cup road fourth from bottom of the Second Division and their new manager just weeks at the Roker controls.

And began it all as so much of an unwanted chore set against the greater need for League points to improve their position.

I heard the end of this tremendous chapter in Roker Park history with Bob Stokoe, lop-side smile and all, standing in the winning Wembley dressing-room saying . . . "*To think that just three months ago we were a bunch of nobodies . . .*"

I was at the start of it all, at the January Third Round meeting with Notts County at Meadow Lane where after a most fortunate draw—they had had to throw Dave Watson forward for one of his headers from a corner to stay alive—I met Bob Stokoe in an empty visiting dressing-room.

There was no elation about that second chance in the replay, just relief.

Remember the circumstances.

He was still very much the new manager feeling his way after only four League and this FA Cup match behind him as the Roker boss. When I ventured that Sunderland had done well to get a replay (against a Third Division side!) Bob was staring into the future and the County again at home come the Tuesday.

TOOK 42 YEARS TO TELL

by
PAT COLLINS

" It gives us another match, keeps up some sort of interest!" he said. " We have got to maintain any extra interest we can, especially in our position, otherwise the season is dead."

Then he went on, still looking through me to Tuesday evening, " It will bring some people back, it's the Cup." And almost as if he were provoking the fates . . . " We could get twenty-five thousand for this at Roker. But the thing is that we are still interested and a good draw, a good name to meet in the Fourth Round, will give us something to go for in this replay."

In the light of what was to follow so dramatically, so unbelievably, as Sunderland ripped off 42 years of Cup history to become the only Second Division club to take the Cup since West Bromwich Albion in 1931, that must provide some small chink of hope for all those once sunlit League clubs now in the shadows. Just to have this to hold onto must be something.

Look at that wonderful revival and what it now means to Sunderland Take such turning-points at other clubs over the last decade and say again that it *CAN* be done . . .

At Liverpool and Leeds . . .

Player-manager Don Revie beginning by peeling off in the Elland Road dressing-rooms to face crowds of 8,000 before he hung up his boots to set about making Leeds United a great power in the world of Soccer.

Bill Shankly doing the same great job at Anfield in around the same time to put the Reds right up at the top, capping it with this last fabulous season that sees his as the first English club to take the League title and a top European prize in the same season.

Remember how Joe Mercer and Malcolm Allison picked Manchester City off the floor. How Arsenal, at long last, got the trophy-touch again. The rise of Derby County under Brian Clough . . .

Leeds, Liverpool, Manchester City and Derby—these have set the success-

Bob Stokoe

MIRACLE-MAN OF ROKER

ful examples that Stokoe and Sunderland will be wanting to emulate. And even proud Anfield itself and the bulging gates there would have competition if they won a glimpse of the one-time golden days at Roker again.

In the time he had and the position he was put in, Bob Stokoe could not have pulled the spotlight more spectacularly round to focus on Sunderland.

He could—and did—win only a respectable table position against the start-to-finish, two-club promotion push by Burnley and Queen's Park Rangers. But in doing any better the slower progression of League affairs could never be anything like as startling a way of selling his club as was the sudden-death and glamour of the Cup.

I said that Bob Stokoe did not dare more than hope for a good draw in the Fourth Round. You'll remember, begging Charlie Hurley's pardon, it was Fourth Division Reading, hardly a plum on the face of it.

But the fates even then bequeathed a thin smile on Stokoe and Sunderland for Reading *DID* provide big Charlie's return to the domain where he had been king as a player.

Stokoe, having got just over a surprising 30,000 for his winning replay against Notts County, saw his side do things the hard way by stumbling at home to Reading and having to win their second replay, this time at Elm Park. All of which meant a mounting interest on Wearside since at long last Sunderland were making things happen.

The interest was shown in gates which, up to Stokoe's arrival, had averaged a little under 13,800. After the Cup defeat of the County and Reading the next two home League games were Millwall (22,781) and Middlesbrough (25,840). It leapt up, of course after the hard-earned draw at Maine Road and then Manchester City's defeat before howling hordes, bringing back so many memories to Roker Park.

Two Cup gates, in fact, which had more than 100,000 packed into the grounds to go along with League crowds which now read: Oxford United (39,222) . . . Carlisle (39,930) . . . Bristol City (33,265) . . .

Following the Cup dismissals of Luton and Arsenal we had Huddersfield (32,251) and Portsmouth (31,431) as soaring to league returns.

By which time the Roker crowd marshals were becoming almost blase.

In the aftermath of Wembley and a Sunderland dressing-room which bulged out at the sides with its enthusiastic winners and still unbelieving visitors, Bob Stokoe meant it when he said: " We had it won before the match ".

He had planned that game right up to the kick-off and beyond, winning all the battles before the actual Wembley war.

Naturally, all uncommitted fans were wishing for a Sunderland success, even if they could not see it happening. Leeds were 11–4 on favourites, had been fighting for the top honours for years, were the actual Cup-holders, but loved by few outside their own followers.

Whereas the TV millions had seen the unashamed Stokoe tears after the semi-final defeat of Arsenal, had seen his fatherly handling of his young side. People were now *WILLING* Sunderland to win.

Bob Stokoe was not one to rely on sentiment alone. He waged a most successful psychological battle over the last few days on behalf of his " underdogs ".

He complained about Leeds getting the better (?) dressing-room, saying it was all cut and dried without his knowledge. He complained about their fans being allotted the end from which both teams emerged from the tunnel—because United would get the boost of a better send-off.

He took his entire team to the annual Football Writers' Association dinner, less than 48 hours before the big show—the man who could trust his young side to act like men before their biggest test.

It was all calculated to tell the world, " Look how we, the underdogs, are facing up to it all ".

His delicately expressed hope that Billy Bremner, the United captain, would be seen but not heard nearly as much as usual on the field, was like slipping a hand-grenade under the match.

To cap it all, he paraded in that red track-suit, just like one of the lads, not to mention having some of his team come RUNNING out for the second half, which just isn't done at Wembley.

Oh yes, Bob Stokoe, fiercely and sincerely as he believed in his side, worked out the angles beforehand, winning all the tricks up to the last

The picture which tells the whole Wembley Cup Final story of 1973 . . . Sunderland's goal brings whoops of joy from Tueart, Guthrie, Watson, scorer Porterfield and the airborne Horswill. And if that 31st minute winner made Porterfield's victory smile even wider it was because his volleyed shot was made with his wrong foot—the right one! Not sharing the rejoicing . . . Leeds' Bremner, keeper Harvey, Clarke and the grounded Hunter. Below: Bremner rides Horswill's tackle and the effort shows on the Sunderland player

seconds in order that his players had just ninety minutes to worry about. Worry? He had somehow cut out even that handicap before they lined up!

In just under six months Stokoe, one-time Newcastle half-back who moved through the managerial ranks by way of Bury, Charlton, who sacked him, Rochdale, Carlisle and Blackpool, had brought back the crowds to Roker Park, given Sunderland their second FA Cup success after 36 years, won a respectable League position and lifted gates to an average of around 22,500, only bettered by Aston Villa in the Second Division.

But more, much more than that, he lifted the grey depression of mediocrity which had settled sullenly over Wear-side for too many long years.

And brought a buoyant hope which sees Roker Park once again a-bustle like it was getting up steam for things to happen.

BILLY HUGHES Sunderland

GOAL GIRL '73

... and Paddy Mulligan crowns yet another Sunderland winner!

ANNE CARTY

'73 is surely Sunderland's year. Anne Carty, 18-year-old art student from Grindon Village, Sunderland, followed the great Roker F.A. Cup Final triumph by becoming GOAL GIRL '73! And here's Anne, in the colours of her Sunderland heroes, receiving congratulations from Eire and Crystal Palace skipper Paddy Mulligan, who performed the crowning ceremony, runner-up (left) Julia Whitbread from Luton and third-place Anne Watson from Ipswich. Anne collected a cheque for £100 for winning the competition outright and another for £50 awarded to the girl footballer (she plays for Rose's Rebels) who finished top of the poll. Julia received a cheque for £50 and Anne Watson one for £25. GOAL GIRL Anne Carty also wins a set of shirts, shorts and stockings for Rose's Rebels from Adidas-Umbro, and the cameraman who took the picture she originally submitted earns a special £50 award from AMATEUR PHOTOGRAPHER.

Ian Porterfield (extreme left) hammers the ball for goal.

A view from another angle—with Porterfield (centre) following up his shot.

I'm the kind of bloke who prefers to recall the good moments football has given me. Like being part of the Second Division shock-troops of Sunderland who carried off last season's F.A. Cup.

But, as I climbed those Wembley steps on that unforgettable day last May to collect my winner's medal, I couldn't help thinking back three years to when my time on Wearside seemed all but over.

I'd been with Sunderland for two years, having signed from Raith Rovers, when I had a disagreement with then manager Alan Brown. From being a first-team regular, I found myself cast into the wilderness. I played just 14 'serious' games in the season '69-70, all of them in the reserves. I wasn't injured, just being punished.

It was an agonising spell. Nine months when I was so fed up and disillusioned I virtually cut myself off from everyone.

And to make matters worse, I had to sit back and watch as the club was relegated from Division One.

I itched to get out there on a Saturday, I felt sure that I could help prevent the 'drop'. But I was just never given the chance.

I finally got so depressed I asked for a transfer. Reluctantly, and only because of professional pride.

I had confidence in my own ability and I wanted to prove that ability with Sunderland and no other club.

There's something special about football on Wearside, I'm a Scot, but football in this corner of England has drawn me closer with each year that has gone by. Yes, even during the bad times.

I can illustrate best how tight a hold football has in this area by describing the amazing scenes that greeted us when we returned to Sunderland with the Cup.

Three hours it took us to cover something like 10 miles from the outskirts of the town on our open-topped bus. Three hours during which it seemed like a million people came out of their homes to cheer us on.

I felt so proud. As an 'outsider' I couldn't help wondering what were the feelings of local lads like Jimmy Montgomery, Ritchie Pitt and Mickey Horswill.

Old folk in wheelchairs, people on crutches, they were all there decked out in red and white, shouting their heads off.

FROM THE SOCCER SCRAPHEAP TO WEMBLEY WINNER!

By

Ian Porterfield

- Sunderland

There is so much to remember about that 'journey of a lifetime.' But perhaps the highlight for me was when the bus passed right by my 'local.'

Outside was a V.I.P. in my life. My Grandfather. My biggest fan and critic.

At 84 he'd travelled to Wembley from his home in Lochgelly to see the final. Now he was there for my welcome back.

The 'old fella' has, in fact seen me play many times since I moved south from Scotland. He saw my first game in red and white against our rivals Newcastle.

We won that day and, do you know, he's never seen me on the losing

Won The Cup For Sunderland

It's there. Leeds keeper Harvey dives in vain.

Scenes of great joy. With scorer Porterfield (second from right) doing some sort of Highland Fling.

After the presentations were over — IAN PORTER-FIELD (left) and his team-mate DENNIS TUEART.

side since. He's been a kind of lucky mascot for the club.

Of course the moment I will always remember is when I achieved what so many players can only dream about, scoring the winning goal in an F.A. Cup final.

I can live it all yet…

My fellow Scot, Billy Hughes, took a corner out on the left. It was a beauty. As it dipped over the heads of half a dozen Leeds players, our centre-forward, Vic Halom, knocked it back towards me

I seemed to have all the time in the world as I controlled it with my left before volleying it past David Harvey, high into the net, with my right foot, the one they all allege I only use for standing on.

And then I was mobbed by my team mates…

Do you wonder, then, that once it was all over, I drank champagne out of the 'right' boot!

It was hard to believe, as we took the field at Wembley, that just six months before, we were the team no-one wanted or cared about.

At the beginning of December we looked as if we were heading for the Third Division. A struggling side, playing before just 10,000 fans and with only one win in 12 matches.

It was then that Bob Stokoe took over as team boss.

A passionate native of the North East, he was 'coming home' to help Sunderland rediscover the heady days they had once known.

But I don't suppose even he imagined he would have such an effect on us that, six months later, we'd walk off with the F.A. Cup.

After the final we attended a magnificent celebration at London's Park Lane Hotel. There were over 500 hundred there. It was a case of backslaps and autographs all night. Just about the only time I stood still was when I was presented with the 'Golden Boot.'

This boot, set in a wooden replica of Wembley, is presented to the player who scores the winning goal. It's valued at £1,000, so I'll need to keep it under guard.

That is just one of the many souvenirs I have of our Cup win. Another is the match ball.

It's the winning captains privilege to keep that particular trophy, but our skipper, Bobby Kerr, decided I should have it for scoring the winning goal.

There is also something else to treasure, a small cup given to me when I arrived back home in Sunderland.

It came from the folk who live in the same road as me on the outskirts of the town Some of the youngsters started it. They thought it would be nice to give me something to remember the great day by.

So they went out, around the doors, collecting donations. Then they bought me this cup.

Wonderful…..

SUNDE

BACK ROW:

ARTHUR COX, VIC HALOM, DICK MALONE, JIM MONTGOMERY, RITCHIE PITT, DAVID WATSON, BOB STOKOE

RLAND

FRONT ROW:

DAVID YOUNG, RON GUTHRIE, BILLY HUGHES, BOBBY KERR, DENNIS TUEART,
IAN PORTERFIELD, MIKE HORSWILL

CHARLES BUCHAN'S
FOOTBALL
SUNDERLAND 1951-1973
Bibliography
&Credits

BIBLIOGRAPHY

Into the Light, Roger Hutchinson - 1999

Soccer from the Press Box, Archie Ledbrooke & Edgar Turner - 1959

Sunderland AFC, The Official History, Paul Days - 1999

The Hamlyn Book of Football Records, Phil Soar - 1981

The History of the Football League, Bryan Butler - 1983

THANKS

As with any book of this detail there have been a great many people involved in all aspects of its creation.

We would like to start by thanking the many organisations who have allowed us to painstakingly work our way through their archives collecting images and topics of interest. We have also received a massive amount of help from ex-players and life-long Albion fans.

With special thanks to:
Simon Meakin, Adele Dolloway

PICTURE CREDITS

Every effort has been made to fulfil requirements with regard to reproducing copyright material.
The publishers will be glad to rectify any omissions at the earliest opportunity.

Images from Goal magazine courtesy of Haymarket Media Group.
Other Images courtesy of Solar Pix, DDP Images Author's own collection.

Charles Buchan's Football Monthly content reproduced with permission from
Max Media Publishing.